"Today's technology has real benefits—and real ... tually anything. Unfortunately, that also makes it easier ... that can change the course of our lives. Jonathan McKee understands the pros and cons of social media, and he offers wise biblical guidance to teens and parents for how to stay safe in this challenging environment."

—Jim Daly, President – Focus on the Family

"This book is so practical! It will definitely be a gift we will give our son when he gets his first device! With a practical question guide, this is a book you can even read with your teenager. From selfies to Snapchat, Jonathan also does a great job of peppering in the truth of the Bible and its timeless advice that can be applied even to our Social Media Culture."

—Maggie John, Co-Host, Senior Executive Producer, 100 Huntley Street

"Jonathan McKee gets that social media for teenagers is not social media: it is just life! In this excellent book, he delves into a topic important to BOTH teens and parents and lays out clear principles for smart online behavior. He doesn't vilify or glorify technology, but instead offers a balanced view on how best to live in a connected world."

—Shaunti Feldhahn, Social Researcher and Best-Selling Author of *For Women Only* and *For Parents Only*

"It's no secret our lives are dominated by technology. This brings great opportunity but also some potential pitfalls. *The Teen's Guide to Social Media* is now my favorite book for helping young people wisely navigate social media. In fact, it's helpful for anyone who uses social media. I could not recommend it more highly."

—Sean McDowell, Ph.D., Biola University Professor, Speaker, and Author of over fifteen books including *A New Kind of Apologist*

"To be honest, I struggled to get through the advanced copy of this book because my teenage sons kept taking it. My boys appreciate Jonathan's candid, comedic, and challenging approach and insist on reading everything he writes. The humor, tips, and wisdom that Jonathan shares here are exactly what young people need and want to hear. Don't let your kid have a mobile device without a copy of this book."

—Pete Sutton, Student Ministry Pastor of Christ Community

"McKee's best yet. This book will most definitely be the new 'phone contract' today's parents use to engage their kids in meaningful conversation about their use of technology. Required reading for any teenager."

—Doug Fields, Author of *Speaking to Teenagers* and *7 Ways to Be Her Hero*

The TEEN'S GUIDE to SOCIAL MEDIA...

& Mobile Devices

21 TIPS TO WISE POSTING IN AN INSECURE WORLD

JONATHAN McKEE

SHILOH RUN PRESS

An Imprint of Barbour Publishing, Inc.

Print ISBN 978-1-68322-319-1

eBook Editions:
Adobe Digital Edition (.epub) 978-1-68322-527-0
Kindle and MobiPocket Edition (.prc) 978-1-68322-528-7

Cover design by Greg Jackson, Thinkpen Design.

The author is represented by, and this book is published in association with, the literary agency of WordServe Literary Group, Ltd., www.wordserveliterary.com.

Published by Shiloh Run Press, an imprint of Barbour Publishing, Inc., P.O. Box 719, Uhrichsville, Ohio 44683, www.shilohrunpress.com.

Our mission is to publish and distribute inspirational products offering exceptional value and biblical encouragement to the masses.

Member of the
Evangelical Christian
Publishers Association

Contents

A Note to Mom or Dad Screening This Book

Walk with Them

*L*et me take a quick moment to say hi to Mom, Dad, Grandma. . .the caring adult who most likely purchased this book for the young person they know and love.

I recognize you!

Seriously. I can spot that facial expression a mile away. I see it every week on the faces of moms, dads, and grandparents at my parent workshops. If there was one word to describe that look, it would probably be *overwhelmed*. It's a mix of fear, frustration, anxiety, care, empathy, caution, and maybe even a dash of anger reserved for those cyberbullies, online predators, and plain ol' mean people who seem so prevalent in today's online village.

Parenting had to be much easier in the '80s, don'tchathink? (My mom and dad might actually contest that.)

As much as we all enjoy our mobile devices, these gadgets are rapidly becoming a source of contention in many homes, maybe because young people are clocking in an average of eight hours and fifty-five minutes per day[1] soaking in entertainment media and technology (or maybe because parents are averaging over nine hours a day[2]). Maybe we've never added up the actual hours and minutes. All we know is that every time we try to open the doors of communication in our home, someone's eyes are glued to a screen.

And even though some of us have contemplated packing

our bags and moving to Ghana, or some safe, faraway location with no Internet or Wi-Fi, we realize our kids will *eventually* get a device, log on, and gain access to the online world (at least, that's what the guy in Ghana holding his smartphone told me).

So maybe we should walk our kids through some tips for the use of this technology.

Perhaps we could give them some information and humble advice as they learn to make decisions for themselves (which they'll be doing in just how many years now?).

As a father of three, I know exactly how you feel, and that's one of the prominent reasons I wrote this little guide. Today's teens and tweens are beginning to make media decisions daily. And most young people are actually open to new information, wisdom, and occasional advice. . .if it's presented candidly for their consideration.

Honestly, weren't we the same way?

Don't tell me what to do. . .but I'll gladly listen to what others have done and decide if that would work for me as well.

That's where this book comes in.

This book provides stories, research, humor, and good common sense about using the phone in your pocket wisely. At times I include scripture where applicable. And I've provided discussion questions at the end of each chapter so that you can dialogue with the reader about what he or she discovers in these pages. Use these questions to engage in meaningful conversation with your kids—not lecturing, but *listening* to what they gleaned from each chapter. Or simply ask them, "What's one thing you discovered in this chapter that might be helpful?"

BUT WHAT ABOUT RULES AND GUIDELINES?

Before you hand a teenager this book, you might have questions about your role. I find today's parents, grandparents, and caring adult role models have very specific questions about raising this generation of kids who have never known life *without* the Internet, phones, and social media.

Here are just some of the questions I hear from parents every week:

- "At what age should my kids get a phone or begin using social media?"
- "Should I use parental controls on their devices?"
- "Should I have the passwords?"
- "Should I limit screen time?"
- "Should we just pack our bags and move to Ghana?"

Let me address these concerns briefly.

The first question is the one I hear the most. "What age should I let my kids have access to all this stuff?" It comes in many forms:

- "How young is too young for my daughter to have her own phone?"
- "I didn't get my son a phone—I just got him an iPad. Is that dangerous?"
- "My eleven-year-old daughter wants an Instagram account. Should I let her?"

Let me give you the quick answer: thirteen years old.

The answer is simple when it comes to social media because most of these platforms require kids to be thirteen to even sign up. If your child tries to sign up for Snapchat, the app will ask for their birth date. If they are under thirteen, it will redirect them to a version called SnapKidz.

Instagram? Thirteen years old.

Facebook? Thirteen years old.

These guidelines exist because of the Children's Online Privacy Protection Act (COPPA), which prevents sites from collecting select information from kids under thirteen.[3] Parents who have allowed their kids to sign up for these apps before thirteen either missed this fact or allowed them to lie about their age.

This should make it much simpler for you when little Emily asks, "Mom, can I have Snapchat?"

"Sorry, Emily, I would let you, but the law doesn't allow me."

I realize saying no to our kids can be difficult when every other parent out there is giving their kids devices before they cut their first tooth. Our kids are sure to complain, "But Brianna has her own iPad!" or "Taylor has had Snapchat forever!"

This is where parents need to stop and ask themselves, "What is my role?" If you want to be the friend-parent or yes-man who gives in to their kid's every whim. . .then by all means, give 'em a phone. But if you see your role as the coach, or Sherpa, who will guide them along the road of adolescence successfully to adulthood, then I recommend you wait until they're twelve or thirteen. And don't let them use social media until the age COPPA allows, which is currently thirteen for most apps.

Does that mean your kids shouldn't have their own phone or iPad until thirteen? Many schools are issuing iPads to kids as early as third or fourth grade. What is a parent to do? Refuse?

Most experts, both liberal and conservative in approach, recommend not giving your kids mobile devices until twelve years old.[4] They actually use the word *devices* instead of *phones* for a reason. If they said "no phones until twelve," then parents would just buy their kids a tablet, an iPod touch, a laptop, or other devices that allow them access to the Internet and social media. And most studies reveal that the majority of parents *don't* use parental controls and *don't* talk about online safety or social media etiquette in any way, so kids are left to fend for themselves. Hence the plea, "Stop giving kids devices!"

Bottom line: It's hard for an eight-year-old to make safe decisions in a world with so many online predators and hazardous distractions (which is why most schools that issue devices issue them with all kinds of "parental controls" and blocks).

So if you (or your kids' school) do decide to give your kids a device, don't just hand it to them and say, "Good luck!" It's necessary to walk *with* them as they get used to their device.

I know, I know! Many of you are thinking, *But they know this device better than I know it!* Still, would you hand your kids the car keys and let them figure out driving by themselves?

I'm not suggesting you hand them a sheet full of rules. I'm suggesting you create a climate of continual conversation about social media and screen entertainment. The best rules, after all, are those that cultivate conversation and equip kids to make decisions. Walk with your kids as they set up their first online profiles, teach them how to use online privacy settings, and give them guidance on who to select as online friends.

When your kids are young, it's okay to start with rigid guidelines. A helpful guideline for a thirteen-year-old with a new phone might be "Talk with Mom or Dad before downloading any new app." This gives you a chance to discuss apps before they venture out into the online world. You can actually set the parental controls on most devices so that young kids can't download apps without parents entering a password (if parents are shrewd enough to come up with a password besides their birthday, anniversary, or street address).

With this kind of guardrail in place, your young kids will always have to come to you and present their case for why they want a specific app, giving you the chance to teach them discernment for when they go through this process on their own.

Some experts advise that parents should know their kids' passwords (especially when they first get their phones) so Mom and Dad can do precisely what the American Academy of Pediatrics recommends[5]: monitoring exactly what websites and social media their kids are using. I think this is a great idea with young kids. Just realize, sometimes demanding a password or scrutinizing your sixteen-year-old's every online move can create a "parent versus teen" dynamic, which is never a good thing. And frankly, I've found if today's kids want to sneak, they will sneak. It's much better to create an environment of fair rules, open communication, and no secrets. So start with rigid guidelines when they're young and slowly segue toward more freedom as they approach the time when they'll be on their own.

I'll be honest. This process of walking with our kids takes time. Good parenting takes time. Those parents who try to lean on rules that will do the parenting for them most often discover. . .it doesn't work. Nothing replaces good ol'-fashioned conversation.

"Dad, I want Instagram."

"Cool. Let's check it out."

And if you *don't* know anything about Instagram, then read

this book with your kid, or Google "Instagram safety tips" or "Instagram privacy settings" and see what people are recommending. Just help your tweens understand these settings; after all, your plan is to equip them with the wisdom and knowledge to choose these kinds of settings when they are on their own in just a few years.

Explain to your child why it's good for a thirteen-year-old to use privacy settings so creepy men sitting in front of a glowing screen in their basement can't see their posts. It's also good to teach them never to friend people they haven't met. Yes, that good-looking eighteen-year-old in Huntington Beach is actually that creepy man in his basement! (Luckily, I'll take them through many of these principles in this book. So if you go through the end-of-chapter discussion questions with them, you'll have a chance to dialogue about many of these issues.)

Engage in regular check-ins, review their privacy settings, and see who their online friends are. Don't be a parole officer, looking for malfeasance. Be a guide, looking to encourage and offer advice where needed.

If your sixteen-year-old grows impatient with these conversations, offer the alternative: Mom and Dad have the passwords and check their phone on demand.

Guess which alternative they'll choose?

Don't get me wrong. This doesn't mean no rules. In fact, one of the rules your family doctor has been recommending for years is limiting screen time.[6] And in a world where young people average almost nine hours per day engaging with entertainment media and technology, this is no easy task. But help your kids avoid falling victim to playing seven hours of video games on a school night. Sit down and talk about some realistic guardrails together and decide what is fair.

One of the best ways to control screen time is by seeking out no-tech zones.

Last year I wrote a helpful book for parents titled *52 Ways to Connect with Your Smartphone Obsessed Kid*. This book was uniquely exciting to write because it is a collection of venues or settings in which parents have successfully engaged in face-to-face communication with their kids. Some of these bonding venues can be created with a simple boundary like "No Tech at the Table." This practice of setting aside all devices before dinner might help keep dinner sacred so that teens aren't staring at their phones and Mom and Dad aren't distracted by their devices either.

These connection venues might be more common than you think. Consider the times when you are driving in the car with your child, or putting them to bed, or sitting down for a meal, and for one reason or another your kid isn't staring at their phone but is truly engaged in meaningful conversation. Sounds like a dream come true, right? If you're a parent today, then you know it can be difficult to get a teen to lift their eyes from their mobile device and actually dialogue. So my advice is simple. Seek out these natural settings where the phone is put away:

- Dinner
- Bedtime
- Sitting in the hot tub
- Exercising
- Hunting, fishing, boating. . .
- Baking (sticky hands and phones don't mix)

Seek out these times when your kids don't really even need

to be told, "Put down your stupid phone!" but naturally start talking.

The world is beginning to wake up to the fact that screens are interfering with relationships at home, with friends, and even with workplace productivity. My friend Curt Steinhorst and I actually just wrote a book on this subject, *Can I Have Your Attention?*, to help leaders overseeing a constantly connected workplace manage a new generation of workers who can't seem to pry their eyes from their devices. We're not alone in recognizing the need for less screen time. Author and leadership consultant Simon Sinek has become very vocal about the need for young adults to just put down their phones and seek out face-to-face connection throughout the day. *New York Times* bestselling author Sherry Turkle has written entire books on the subject. Each of these experts recognizes and identifies emerging problems with constant connectivity and suggests ways to reclaim conversation.

Your family doctor has even chimed in on this need to occasionally distance ourselves from technology. As I write this, the American Academy of Pediatrics just released its new list of media tips for parents,[7] and several of the tips encourage parents to "create tech-free zones" and "seek out face-to-face time." Experts are realizing how important it is for parents to set aside their devices and simply seek out one-on-one time.

When you start reading the research, it's a little scary exactly how damaging a smartphone is becoming to a generation of young people who barely know life without it. How will they ever learn responsibility if we don't teach them?

Guess who has the best opportunity to teach this?

Guess who can best model this?

You don't need to pack up your family and move to Ghana.

Just look for opportunities to engage in meaningful dialogue with your kids. My hope is that this book will be a catalyst for those conversations.

If you would like to read more about walking with our kids and teaching them to make wise media decisions, Jonathan devotes an entire chapter to the subject in his most recent parenting book, If I Had a Parenting Do-Over, *a book providing real-world examples of media guidelines for various ages.*

A Note to You

Your Phone Is Not the Problem

Confession: I love my phone!

There. I said it. Let the record show, I think the gadget in my pocket is resourceful, efficient. . .and fun!

I travel a lot, and honestly, life would be way more difficult without my phone!

On a travel day, when I get up, I open my airline's app to see if my flight is on time. Then I check my rental car app and my hotel app.

Sweet! I'm driving a Mini Cooper today! (Free upgrades rock!)

Then I'll pop on social media (sometimes from the bathroom—shut up—you know you do it!) usually to check in on a couple of friends and to post about an article or something I read.

I'll check the news feed at breakfast (because no one else is up in my house at 4:00 a.m.), and when I get into my car, I'll turn on one of my favorite music playlists. Actually, I typically jump on that same free music-streaming app you use and pull up one of my daughter's playlists and listen to hers. She has *waaaaay* better taste than me.

When I arrive at the airport, I use my phone to see what gate I'm at, then I pull up my boarding pass.

How many apps is that already?

And that's not even counting the app I used at the airport yesterday when I heard a song I liked but couldn't remember who sang it. Thanks to my phone, I learned the song and artist in less than ten seconds.

How cool is that?

And that's just my phone activity before I boarded at 5:30 a.m. Imagine the rest of my day. (I watched a movie on my phone in-flight.)

So please understand, I'm not about to tell you that your phone is bad. Phones aren't the problem. People just make bad decisions with their phones.

People make bad decisions with cars also. They get in the car when drunk or angry and they speed, endangering the lives of everyone in their path. Robbers, murderers, and pedophiles use cars. Some use them to help their crimes! Does this make cars "bad"? Last year alone, 38,300 people in the US died in motor vehicle accidents![1] Cars are actually the number one killer of teenagers![2] It's true. Look at any "mortality report" about deaths in America, and you'll find that about half of teen deaths are caused by "accidents," about three-quarters of which are in motor vehicles. Nothing else comes close.

If that many cars are killing teenagers, should we ban the use of cars?

Are cars all-out bad?

Just wait a minute—simmer down, now.

What if we try to discover why young people are dying in cars and seek to correct the cause? Experts have noted that teenage drivers are more likely than adults to speed, follow other cars too closely, and drive too aggressively.[3] Not to mention that driving drunk, messaging while driving, and driving with a bunch of distracting friends are all leading causes of accidents. Maybe that's why our country has created laws focused on eliminating these risky behaviors.

It might have seemed unfair to you when your state enforced a law declaring you can't drive alone with friends until you're older. It might be inconvenient when you *can't* check those incoming texts or messages while driving. But these laws have saved countless lives.

Hear what I'm saying. After all, I'm advocating for you. I'm telling you, cars are *not* the problem. We just need to learn to drive responsibly. In the same way, your phone is *not* the problem. Just learn to use your phone responsibly.

Your phone is a handy little device that can bring knowledge, provide convenience, and help you communicate with others. At the same time, your phone can distract you from what's important and damage your relationships with the people around you.

It's your choice how you want to use it.

SMARTER THAN YOUR SMARTPHONE

The name isn't misleading. It's a smart little phone. You just have to be smart with it. That's the purpose of this book, to help you make good decisions, not just on your phone but on all of your mobile devices.

The phone is causing quite a stir in a lot of homes. In fact, 66 percent of parents feel their kids spend too much time on their phones.[4]

What do you think?

Do you think you spend too much time on your phone? Because 52 percent of teenagers agree with their parents and feel that today's young people spend too much time on their phones. In fact, 50 percent of teenagers say they feel like they are actually "addicted" to their devices.[5]

Are you enslaved to your phone?

Could you do without it?

Apparently it's not just teenagers who are addicted to their devices. Some parents are, too. An Illinois woman was home with her teenage daughter when their house caught fire. Luckily both were able to escape as flames literally engulfed the house.

Then the mom realized she left her phone in the house.

True story: The mom ran back into the house to grab it and wasn't able to escape the flames a second time.[6]

Do you really need your phone *that bad*?

Consider what I tell kids at school assemblies across the nation: "Phones can be great tools, but they are a lousy crutch."

If I snatched your phone away, would you fall on your face?

Chances are, you aren't tech-dependent. Sure, it might feel like it at times, but honestly, think of the last time you lost a signal to your device for over an hour.

You survived!

It's true—you can actually communicate with your friends without your phone. In fact, in the pages of this book you'll discover you can actually communicate *better* when you are face-to-face with your friends and your phone is tucked away neatly in your pocket.

Researchers have done studies to test exactly how much the smartphone is affecting people's ability to connect with each other in person. Guess what they found?

- A study out of the University of Essex revealed that the mere presence of a phone in face-to-face settings had negative effects on the connection people felt and the quality of their conversation.[7]
- In a study titled "The iPhone Effect," researchers noted, "Conversations in the absence of mobile communication technologies were rated as significantly

superior compared with those in the presence of a mobile device."[8]

- The same study reported, "People who had conversations in the absence of mobile devices reported higher levels of empathetic concern."

In simple terms: You actually communicate better when you put down your phone, look someone in the eye, and have a normal face-to-face conversation.

Your phone isn't the problem. The problem is when people let the phone interfere with their communication.

Do you know what that means?

You are smarter than your smartphone.

Your smartphone is a helpful little tool, but that's all it is. A tool.

Don't be a tool.

Own a tool.

And if you feel like a tool, enslaved to social media and your devices, my hope is that this book will help you move from being *tech-dependent* to becoming *tech-enabled*.

It all starts with you.

KNOW YOURSELF

Jimi Hendrix, notably one of the greatest guitar players of all time, once said, "Knowledge speaks, but wisdom listens."[9]

Powerful words. Wisdom is available to those of us who are teachable.

I'd like to make an agreement with you. I promise in the pages of this book that I'll present you with relevant research and real stories. I'm *not* going to tell you what to do. You're the one who has to make these choices. My goal is to provide you with information and then let you make choices based on that information.

I'm asking you for only one thing: *honesty.*

You'll get the most out of this book when you look at yourself honestly.

Here's why I mention this. This topic of social media and technology is very sensitive for some people. It can sometimes put people on the defensive. When they read something about people spending too much time on their phones, their instinctive response is, *"I don't spend too much time!"* I even hear adults respond that way when they hear information that hits a little too close to home. They don't want to listen.

So I ask you simply to evaluate the information at hand. Who knows, maybe you don't spend too much time staring at your devices. But what if you do, and it's affecting your relationships with the people you care about most? If so, wouldn't you like to recognize the signs?

Aristotle said, "Knowing yourself is the beginning of all wisdom."[10]

I promise never to accuse you personally of anything. But I will frequently write, "Research shows that young people. . ." or tell a relevant story on the topic. And I'll also ask you honestly, "Is this a struggle for you?" If it is, then I'll give you some helpful tips to free yourself from that particular struggle. I'll even include scripture to provide some time-tested wisdom on the matter.

And honestly, a lot of what you'll discover in these pages isn't even about young people as much as it is about dangerous adults out there you need to be aware of. Some adults aren't proving to be very responsible with their social media and technology, making wise device use that much more difficult for young people. Hopefully the information in this book will help you steer clear of those dangers and distractions.

After all, you're smarter than your smartphone.

So how can you make wise choices in such an insecure world?

Let's dive in.

21 Tips
TO WISE POSTING
IN AN
INSECURE WORLD

Tip #1

Love the one you're with.
Discovering the secret of "social" in a social media world

It wasn't uncommon to see our family room packed with kids. My three kids would each invite their friends, and before we knew it, we had kids bouncing off the walls. The more kids, the higher the volume. My kids were loud!

Then they became teenagers.

You'd think teenagers would be louder. . .right?

I remember a particular day when we had about half a dozen teenagers over. As each of them arrived I'd hear voices raised in excitement, but then the volume would decrease. I could hear it all from where I was sitting in my office down the hall.

Finally, when all of them settled in the family room together, I noticed the house had grown quiet—deathly quiet. Literally silent. I thought, *Did they all leave? I didn't even hear them go.*

I walked into the front room, and there they all were sitting on our big sectional couch.

I don't even have to tell you why they were silent, do I?

There were seven people in the room and not a single one of them was talking. They were all engrossed in their phones.

I leaned over my daughter's shoulder to look at her screen. She was texting the guy on the opposite end of the couch.

I did what we dads often do. I stated the obvious.

"He's right there!" I said, pointing to my daughter's boyfriend.

She didn't like that very much.

The ironic thing is, she ended up breaking up with the guy a few weeks later because—guess what—he wasn't really good at talking. This guy would text my daughter and connect with her through social media consistently, but when the two of them got together, he was awkward and silent.

Have you ever met someone like this?

It's because *social* media is destroying our ability to be *social*.

ANTI-SOCIAL MEDIA

In a world where 89 percent of teenagers report using some type of social media, you'd think young people would be more. . .*social*.[1] In actuality, it's quite the opposite.

The evidence is clear. Face-to-face conversations are becoming much more difficult for young people today. People are spending far more of their waking hours staring at screens than they are communicating face-to-face. . .and it's inhibiting their ability to have a conversation.

As people become more used to screens, they struggle to maintain dialogue with real-life people. You probably don't need to read a study to come to that conclusion. If you go to school or have any contact with other young people day to day, then you've probably noticed these symptoms:

- Someone pulling out a phone and looking at it in the middle of a face-to-face conversation
- Someone who is very chatty through screens but proves to be quite the opposite in person
- A failure to understand (or even recognize) what others are actually feeling and experiencing
- Screen time distracting people from important tasks

- A decrease in face-to-face social time as screen time increases

In short, as those of today's "smartphone generation" become more screen-dependent, they are becoming socially impaired.

We're seeing this trend reveal itself in several different ways.

1. Diminished Ability to Recognize Facial Expressions

The more time young people spend communicating through screens, the less they recognize real-life face-to-face "social cues." In other words, they don't even know what "worried" looks like on someone's face.

A few years ago, UCLA did an eye-opening study where they sent a group of kids to an outdoor camp for five days. This was no ordinary camp. The kids who attended were unplugged and media-free for all five days. No phones, no Internet, no music, no TV. . .nothing!

The researchers observed these kids, comparing them to another group of kids who were connected and plugged in to a normal media diet. By the end of the five days, the unplugged kids were better able to understand emotions and nonverbal cues than the plugged-in kids.[2]

Let that sink in for a moment.

After kids spent only five days talking, laughing, and interacting with each other face-to-face, they were able to communicate better. They could actually recognize and differentiate when a friend was content, stressed, excited, or scared.

This should give us hope. Who cares if the majority of young people are becoming screen-dependent. You can be a better listener—and a better friend—when you simply put your phone in your pocket while hanging out with your friends.

Many of us are resistant to putting our phones away. In fact, as digital communication becomes more mainstream, we've even come up with new tools to try to duplicate face-to-face interaction. We use emojis to try to help our friends "see" our mood. We snap pics of our facial expression as we message each other. And these help. . .a little bit.

Some social researchers decided to measure exactly how effective these different kinds of communication are through a unique bonding experiment where people engaged in conversation with friends in four different ways: in person, video chat, audio chat, and instant messaging. Bonding was measured and was found to differ "significantly across the conditions."[3]

As much as people love texting and want it to be effective, instant messaging failed to relay many of the intended facial expressions and voice inflections. Even when texters tried using ALL CAPS or emojis, it proved to be the *least effective* method of all four types of communication. In fact, the greatest bonding occurred during the in-person interaction, followed by video chat, audio chat, and finally instant messaging.

My oldest daughter, Alyssa, who loves texting, once told me, "I never use texting for deep conversations. If you ever get in a fight with your friend or your boyfriend, put the phone down and drive over to their house to work it out. Texting is the worst way to work things out. You can't tell if they're mad, sad, or truly over it. Always do your deep communicating face-to-face."

I think Alyssa is onto something. Digital mediums are handy (I love them), but they lose something. In fact, another negative by-product many are noticing is. . .

2. Lack of Empathy

The more we stare at screens, the less likely we are to "empathize" with our friends.

Empathy is our ability to step into someone else's shoes and consider how they feel. Experts are discovering a strong connection between technology and a lack of empathy. This goes way beyond a diminished ability to recognize others' facial expressions. Not only are we missing what they're communicating, but *we've stopped caring*. The lack of understanding has created a lack of empathy.

Sherry Turkle, MIT professor and author of the book *Reclaiming Conversation: The Power of Talk in a Digital Age*, has observed this in her own research, noting today's kids "don't seem to be able to put themselves in the place of other children." In fact, kids who are sitting around staring at their phones consistently "seem to understand each other less."[4]

In short, people are becoming more self-absorbed. *I care about you less because I'm so caught up in my own world.*

This lack of empathy is hurting relationships. Who wants to hang out with someone who is only into himself? In the same way, who wants to hang out with someone who is so engrossed in their phone all the time that they don't even recognize what you're feeling?

Sadly, the natural next step in this digression is. . .

3. A Decrease in Close Friends

Social media isn't just making conversation more difficult; it's actually killing our close relationships.

Most research suggests that the more time a young person spends dialoguing with people through their screens, the fewer friends they have. This might seem counterintuitive, but think about it for a moment. The progression makes sense:

- People today are spending more time on screens than at any other time in history.
- The more time people spend communicating through screens, the less effectively they communicate face-to-face.
- People are spending less time communicating face-to-face since it's difficult.
- The decrease in face-to-face communication is leading to a lack of empathy for others—people who are self-absorbed.
- No one likes to be around someone who is self-absorbed.
- People have fewer close friends.

Just last month UCLA developmental psychologist Patricia Greenfield reported young people are seeking social support through social media, and "the result is a decline in intimate friendships."[5] The more young people turn to e-friends, the less they turn to face-to-face friends. The result is fewer close friends.

Social media is making us less social.

IN YOUR POCKET

You have the power to reverse this trend within your circle of friends. You don't have to smash your smartphone. You don't have to give up streaming Netflix. Your phone isn't the problem. In fact, the solution is simple: just put your phone in your pocket when you're hanging out with your friends and family.

Your phone is a great tool for connecting with people

outside the room. . .when it doesn't sever your connection with the people inside the room!

It's a simple matter of respect. Maybe you've had the frustrating experience of sharing your heart with a friend and they keep checking their phone while you talk. You just wanna say, "Sorry, am I interrupting something *more important*?"

If you don't want to be treated this way, don't treat others that way.

It's called "the Golden Rule."

Actually, the Golden Rule is from the Bible. It's something Jesus said in the book of Matthew: "Do to others whatever you would like them to do to you. This is the essence of all that is taught in the law and the prophets" (Matthew 7:12).

Imagine that. Think about what it would look like if everyone walked through life considering others first. What would that be like at school? What about at home?

Picture your friend putting away their phone when you walk into the room, looking up at you, asking you about your day, and truly listening to you when you talk. *Really* listening, like they're interested! (Hopefully you have some friends who actually do this.)

If that sounds good to you, then Jesus is simply asking you to do the same to your friends.

What could that look like this week?

QUESTIONS TO PONDER

1. Have you ever spent time with someone who was glued to their phone, even when you were trying to hang out with them? How did you feel?

2. Have you ever done that with a friend? With a parent?

3. Why do you think the "unplugged" kids in the UCLA

study mentioned above were better able to understand emotions and nonverbal cues than the plugged-in kids after just five days without any phones or media?

4. Why do you think kids who are sitting around staring at their phones consistently "seem to understand each other less"?

5. Why does someone who is self-absorbed have fewer friends?

6. What is Jesus' simple advice to us about the way to treat others?

7. What did He mean when He said this advice was the "essence" of all that was taught in the Bible up to that point? How important is that?

8. I asked it at the end of this chapter, but let me ask it again: What is a way you can "do to others what you would like them to do to you" this week?

9. Google the word "empathize." What does it mean? How can you live that out this week?

SOMETHING TO THINK ABOUT

The MIT professor I mentioned earlier in this chapter made an interesting observation about the effect of smartphones on people's relationships: "Studies of conversation both in the laboratory and in natural settings show that when two people are talking, the mere presence of a phone on a table between them or in the periphery of their vision changes both what they talk about and the degree of connection they feel."[6]

Think about that for a moment. A guy and a girl are having dinner. The guy pulls out his phone and puts it on the table. The phone buzzes and the screen lights up throughout the meal. If the guy looks at it, he has just revealed his priorities:

The communication coming from the phone is more important than the communication here at the table. If the guy *doesn't* look at it. . .why is the phone even on the table?

Try something. Keep your phone in your pocket during meals with friends or family, and see if it becomes contagious. Look them in the eye during conversation. Give them your full attention. You'll find these kinds of proactive efforts to communicate with others are often reciprocated—people will do the same back to you. But if you find you're the only one who *doesn't* have their phone out, consider announcing this: "Let's try something. Everyone put your phone in the center of the table. First one to grab their phone has to do dishes/pay for the bill!"

Who knows? You might start a trend.

The smartphone is a great tool to connect with people outside the room, but only when it doesn't interfere with our relationships with the people inside the room.

Tip #2

*I*t was only a few months after her high school graduation when she got into the car with two of her friends that night in a small town in Washington State. She rode shotgun.

Both of her friends put on their seatbelts.

For some reason, she didn't.

The crash shouldn't have been a big deal. The belts saved the other two, but she was ejected from the vehicle and killed instantly.

It happens all the time; not to every kid or even every family, but every city has a story of a car wreck and the one person who didn't make it because they weren't wearing their seatbelt. Seatbelts save over two thousand lives a year.

That's probably why car companies, starting way back in January 1, 1968, were required by law to provide seatbelts in all seating positions. It wasn't until 1983 that laws kicked in to require people to actually wear them.[1]

People whined and complained when this law was enforced. And there is always that one guy who will claim, "Yeah, but I heard you're safer without your belt! I've heard of someone being thrown from the car and that's what saved them!" (Something you'll never see on *MythBusters*.)

That's just like us. If it's inconvenient, then we complain about it.

Until it saves our life.

It was New Year's Eve and my cousin asked me if I wanted to go for a ride in his new BMW. I got into the car with him, and he began showing me "what the car could do." Next thing I knew, we were going over 70 miles an hour down a rural road.

I was growing concerned as he kept looking away from the road. He was more focused on the car's features than actually driving (something we'll talk about in greater detail later in the book).

"That's the automatic temperature control, that's the seat-back adjustment, and that's the subwoofer control. . ."

As he was messing with the radio trying to show me the voice commands, he began drifting to the side of the road.

The next few seconds seemed to happen in slow motion.

When he felt his wheel riding on the shoulder of the road, he looked up and turned the wheel sharply, overcorrecting toward oncoming traffic. After barely missing an oncoming car, he cranked the wheel back to try to regain control.

I don't remember the next sixty seconds.

We woke up on the side of the road upside down.

We were both wearing our seatbelts.

Apparently my cousin had cranked the wheel so hard at such a high speed that he flipped the car. We rolled several times and ended up in the ditch backward. The airbags never deployed.

When we took off our seatbelts, our inverted bodies dropped to the roof of the car—now the floor. As we crawled out of the car, unscathed, my cousin merely pointed to the underside of the car and said, "And that's the bottom of the car."

Nobody likes safety features. . .until they protect you!

I KNOW WHERE YOU LIVE

A forty-four-year-old Los Angeles man was arrested last year for using the location information from people's Facebook and Instagram photos to break into people's homes and steal their underwear.[2]

Yeah. True story. There is no way I could make this stuff up.

The man used several different methods. His favorite was hanging out in public places and waiting for people to "check in" on Facebook. Once he found someone of interest, he would follow their posts and look for clues as to where they lived. He also used this method to find people on Instagram and other social media apps. He simply looked for people who posted pictures with locations, then followed the GPS information to figure out where they lived. Then he would break into their house and steal their underwear. . .sometimes just feet away from where they were sleeping.

Creepy!

The only reason he was able to do this was because these people didn't make use of their privacy settings.

PRIVACY SETTINGS

Have you ever used or adjusted your privacy settings on your phone and other devices?

Remember when you first got your phone? What about when you downloaded your first app? Do you even remember looking at the privacy settings for any of your devices and/or social media accounts?

Privacy settings are one of those important safety standards that people *don't* pay much attention to. I understand why. Every day we are so bombarded with information that we experience "data overload." It's a natural response to begin ignoring some of it. Historically speaking, social media is relatively new. And we certainly haven't had it in our pockets for long. It wasn't until 2012 that the majority of people in the US owned smartphones. So really our world is just beginning to figure out some of this stuff. Your phone is like a 1962 GM car that came equipped with the metal connectors for seatbelts (called anchor plates) *only* if the particular US state required them. Some states did and some didn't. It took awhile for people to realize how much we actually needed them. People ignored seatbelts for literally decades.

In the same way, many of us choose to ignore privacy settings. *Ain't nobody got time for that!* They're like commercials. Just skip them. Even if a social media account asks us important questions, we often miss them. For example: Do you know that you have to be thirteen years old to have an Instagram account? If you already have an Instagram account, do you remember Insta asking you your age?

Most of us don't remember or even pay attention to these details. We just click "Agree" twenty-seven times so we can begin posting pics. And some creepy, fat, naked guy staring at a glowing screen in his basement in Wisconsin loves that you didn't pay attention to those details, because now he can look at the pictures you just posted of your slumber party with all your friends.

And if you don't appreciate me bringing up the fact that this particular creepy guy is naked. . .good! I'm glad that makes you uncomfortable. It should. I promise you he's real. Google "sex offenders in my area" and look at the map (don't use a site that requires you to enter your e-mail—a good "privacy" practice). These guys are everywhere, and they aren't always fat and creepy looking. Sometimes they are skinny and surprisingly good-looking, yet pedophiles just the same.

WISE PRIVACY PRACTICES

Privacy settings are free tools that help you connect with the people you want and keep out the people you don't.

Take a few seconds to pull up the privacy settings on your devices and social media accounts. No, seriously, pull them up. I'll wait. You'll find it worth your time. Below I've listed some common safety practices to consider.

(Note: I can't give you specifics for how to set your privacy settings for each device and app you use; they vary by device and are updated continually. You'll have to do a bit of clicking around to discover them. Most apps have a "Settings" tab or drop-down that allows you to set controls for who is allowed to see you.)

1. Privacy Settings Enabled

Whenever you download a new app, immediately enable the privacy settings. It might be one of those initial boring questions the device asks you. Pay attention. Those few seconds could save you a world of grief. And if you already have the app, just go back in and take a look at those settings now. One important setting to consider is. . .

2. Friends Only

Don't let any random person "friend" you or gawk at the pictures you just posted. Seriously consider letting only people you know look at your posts and have access to your information. So find a place in your privacy settings to adjust who sees your stuff. It's good to choose just the people you have chosen as *friends*. If you choose *friends of friends*, then you're letting all the friends of your four hundred friends look at you. Ask yourself, "Are all four hundred of my friends making good choices about who they choose as friends?" Probably not. Chances are, at least one of your friends friended creepy basement guy without even knowing it. Choosing "friends only" leaves the discretion to you.

3. Location Settings Turned Almost Completely Off

"Location" settings tell people where you are. This feature is pretty cool when you lose your phone. Then you can use features like "Find My iPhone" to figure out where you left it. But if you aren't careful, your location settings will also tell that same creepy guy in the basement where you are. Trust me, you want him to stay in his basement.

Keep your location settings on for your device overall, but turn them off in each of your individual apps. This is especially important on your phone since you carry it with you. So in Snapchat, for example, you might consider adjusting "who can see my location" under settings and choosing "Ghost Mode" or at least handpicking only select, trusted friends who will see you in Snap Maps.

Where can you adjust the location settings on your devices? On the iPhone you go into your settings and look for the "Privacy" option. Then you'll see "Location Services." On my friend's android, he went to his phone's settings, clicked the "General" tab, and found a setting simply called "Location." Again, it varies by device, but with a little clicking around you'll find it. I recommended my daughters keep their location settings *on* overall, but then scroll down to each app and turn them off individually. Some users don't like turning off their locations because doing so prevents them from posting their location with their pic. If you must have this feature, decide if you're responsible enough to remember *not* to post locations when you're vulnerable, like when you're studying late at a coffee shop and you post a picture of your new mug before calling it a night. Now the basement guy knows where you are and that you're going to your car soon. (Think about that for a moment.)

You'll have to consider these ramifications for every app. Maybe even ask the advice of someone you respect.

And remember, never post a location when you're home. It only takes one picture to let everyone know where you live. That means if you use something like Facebook Places, don't "check in" at home. Some people think they're being sly by not mentioning it, but then they mention everywhere else that they "aren't home." You'd be surprised how many people take pictures getting ready—even in their bathroom—*and leave the location settings turned on.* Uh. . .your makeup, hair spray, and blow dryer are all in the pic. People know that's your own bathroom; it's obviously not a Taco Bell bathroom! Rule of thumb: Never check in at home or post any pics with locations at home. (Or maybe stop posting pics from your bathroom!)

If you've already posted from home with your location settings on, delete any of those posts. . .and lock your doors and windows.

4. No Signing in with Social Media

Sometimes when you are signing up for something, it will give you the option to sign in with social media. Avoid this. When you log in with Facebook or Twitter, it often is giving this new entity access to all your friends, posts, and information. If you absolutely feel you must do this, then read the fine print. Are you allowing them access to your contacts and other data? Are your friends going to hate you for allowing Billy Bob's Country Music Mix to start bothering them and asking them to subscribe to their music service?

Have you looked at your privacy settings?

QUESTIONS TO PONDER

1. Why do you think people don't wear seatbelts? Is it worth it?
2. Over half of parents never talk with their kids about privacy settings. Why do you think this is?
3. Have you ever given out your information or access to your data and regretted it later?
4. Did any of these recommended privacy practices make you think twice? Which ones?
5. Who will you allow to "see your stuff"?
6. What might you need to adjust in your location controls? Why?
7. Who is a trusted adult you can talk with about these kinds of choices? When will you connect with them next?

SOMETHING TO THINK ABOUT

Privacy settings might be a little inconvenient. So are seatbelts. But they both save lives.

Take a few moments to jump into your privacy settings today. Are these controls set in a way that keeps you and the others in your house safe?

Don't make it easy for "basement guy."

Tip #3

Nothing you post is temporary.
Ever wish you could "unpost" something?

a sixteen-year-old girl had a crush on a guy at her school. He asked her to send a nude photo on Snapchat. After all, the picture isn't permanent, right? (We'll spend a lot of time talking about that in Tip #10, my chapter about Snapchat.) She really liked the guy, so after repeated requests, she finally gave in.

It was only a matter of days before the whole school had seen the photo. She couldn't even walk the hallways without hearing whispers, giggles, and even bold comments thrown in her face.

The guy had used special software to download the picture without her knowledge and sent it to a group of friends. Those friends showed friends, and before long, "everyone" had seen it.[1]

The story isn't unique. In fact, you've probably heard a similar story or even experienced this kind of situation as a bystander. That's because the popularity of sending nudes or "sexy pics" is only growing, and since relationships in which people send nudes typically don't last, it's not unusual to see someone send those images to a bunch of their friends in an act so common it now has a name: *revenge porn*.

Sometimes these pics are even taken without a person's knowledge. In some instances, a "friend" takes pictures of their friend changing at home or in the locker room, then posts those pics. These people aren't thinking through the long-term effects of such an impulsive decision. They are hurting someone else. . .for a long time!

People still haven't learned that once you click "Post" or "Send," it's out there, and you can't get it back.

It's not just sexy pics that come back to haunt people. (We'll talk more about this later as well.) All kinds of words and images you post leave a lasting impression on family, friends, and potential bosses. Yeah! Bosses. Consider that example seriously, because according to a recent edition of Jobvite's annual Social Recruiting Survey, 93 percent of hiring managers will evaluate a job candidate's social media profile before hiring them.[2] Yes. When you want a good job somewhere other than that burger shack down the street, your potential boss will most likely check your social media profiles. And in this recent survey of all those bosses, these were the posts that scared them away:

- In the survey, 83 percent of recruiters said mentioning or even joking about using illegal drugs is a strong turn-off.
- Foul language offended the majority.
- 70 percent said sexual posts would count against you.
- Over half of potential bosses didn't like seeing posts about guns.
- 44 percent didn't like seeing any posts with alcohol.
- 66 percent said spelling and grammar were a huge factor.
- One in six didn't like people posting about their political affiliation.[3]

Bottom line: When you post a picture or a rant on social media, it leaves a lasting impression! So be careful what you post.

Once it's out there. . .*it's out there.*

I don't want to try to scare you, but as a social researcher who spends a lot of time studying trends in youth culture, let me just tell you that I've encountered literally hundreds, if not thousands, of stories of young people who posted a pic just once in the moment, only to have that image haunt them for the rest of their lives. The one comment I've read over and over again is, "I wish I could go back and undo that moment."

The same is true of the words you type. People think they are safe because they're on a website that claims anonymity. Don't be fooled. This isn't a badge of protection, and your identity isn't as hidden as you thought. Authorities legally access conversations and expose real identities all too often, especially when someone has been threatened or endangered. In each of these situations, the accused always squeals, "I thought this was anonymous!"

In addition, hackers illegally access people's conversations frequently. (Remember WikiLeaks?) The person who has something to hide always barks and complains, "I thought this was a private conversation!"

And even in normal everyday teen life, young people have conversations they thought were private, only to discover later they were overheard, recorded, screenshotted, or simply copied and shared without permission.

Sometimes young people even tell me, "I accidentally sent a snap to the wrong person. I had to text them and beg them not to open it."

I always ask them, almost rhetorically, "What would you honestly do if someone asked you *not* to open a snap?"

Exactly!

Once you type it, people can swipe it. So don't type it or

click it if you don't want everyone seeing it.

If there's one piece of advice computer and social media experts will tell you over and over again, it's this: *Nothing you post is temporary.*

PROTECTING YOURSELF

I've frequently heard social media experts advise, "Always be careful what you allow someone to film." Personally, I don't think this is very good advice, simply because I've read countless stories of people who didn't even realize they were being filmed or recorded.

Here's a better piece of advice: Live your life in such a way that people can't accuse you of anything.

Yeah. You read that correctly.

What I'm suggesting is, don't get drunk, don't make racial slurs, don't smoke a bowl, don't get naked with anyone but your spouse. And guess what? Then you'll never have to worry, "Is there a camera in this room?"

Honestly, it's not my advice. It comes from a guy named Peter in the Bible. Peter messed up countless times, but after he came to know Jesus and spent a lot of time with Him, his life was completely transformed. In the book of 1 Peter he wrote, "It is God's will that your honorable lives should silence those ignorant people who make foolish accusations against you" (1 Peter 2:15).

That advice is a lot different than "Be careful what people film you doing." Peter is saying, "Be careful how you *live*."

Wouldn't it be nice if we were living our lives in such a way that we never had to worry, "I hope someone didn't record that!"

QUESTIONS TO PONDER

1. Is sending nudes a common occurrence at your school or among young people in your area?

2. Have you ever known someone who sent or received a nude pic? What happened?

3. How often have you encountered someone you know posting *anything* inappropriate?

4. Why do you think these people aren't worried about these posts coming back to haunt them?

5. What are some of the common ways you think inappropriate posts come back to haunt people?

6. What advice does Peter give us for how we should live our lives?

7. What does an "honorable life" look like on social media today?

8. How does living an honorable life silence accusers?

9. Do you need to make any adjustments in what you post? Give an example.

SOMETHING TO THINK ABOUT

I don't know anyone who is perfect. I'm sure not. Most of us probably have made our fair share of mistakes.

Making mistakes is one thing, but making a conscious decision to get drunk, get naked with someone, or spew hateful speech is an entirely different matter. And in a world with cameras everywhere, such decisions have a very high chance of being posted permanently.

So save yourself a lot of trouble and avoid these kinds of activities. And definitely be careful what you post. Whenever you post something, post it knowing that your grandma, your future boss, *and Jesus* are reading every word and looking at the pictures. After all, even if your boss misses it, a day is coming when all that is secret will be brought into the open (Luke 8:17).

Tip #4

The whole picture of those pictures.
A deeper look at the effects of porn

*I*t started with a simple Google image search.

He was adding a few last-minute touches to his speech for French class and needed one more slide. He typed in some keywords and began scanning the images for a high-res pic he could use.

That's when he saw it.

He instinctively looked over his shoulder to see if anyone else was in the living room. His parents were gone and his sister was still at soccer practice. He was completely alone.

He stared at the image. It wasn't pornographic per se, but it was pretty close. He knew he shouldn't click on it, but he was. . .*curious*. He wrestled with the decision. *Why should I deny myself a little bit of eye candy? What possible harm could come from looking at a few pictures?*

That's the way it begins with many porn addicts. They never even fathom the possibility of becoming "addicted," but that's exactly what happens. Before they know it, they can't last but a few days without accessing sexual imagery on one of their many screens. Then once a day. Sometimes more frequently than that. Soon they are literally enslaved to pornography, and it seeps into every area of their lives.

Why is pornography such a struggle for so many?

We live in a world where sexual imagery flashes before our eyes at every click. It doesn't matter if we're thumbing through stories on our phone or watching Sunday night football on the big screen: sexual imagery is there. And the world seems to think this bombardment of sensual images is no big deal.

Is it?

The characters on our favorite TV show joke about it. Creative memes featuring the message "send nudes" go viral. It's all a big joke, right?

Then why does seeing these images, even in mild forms, often open the door to looking at more explicit pictures?

It's brain chemistry 101. Sexy images trigger the release of dopamine, the neurotransmitter in our brain that gives us a feeling of exciting pleasure. People enjoy this feeling, so they seek it out again and again viewing porn. When a person does this often enough, the brain begins rewiring itself and requires more stimuli to get the same excitement. So people will start searching out more graphic or even "weirder" porn to get the same thrill. Porn leads to more porn.[1]

This problem has grown astronomically in the last decade with the increased accessibility of high-speed Internet making porn so readily available. Most studies reveal that of regular visitors to porn sites, about two-thirds are guys and about one-third are girls. Both are experiencing consequences, but on very different levels.[2]

For guys, regular porn viewing actually can affect their ability to perform sexually once they get into a relationship. Once they get to that special sexual encounter with the one they love, they can't get everything working. Or, to use the term you learned in your sex education class, they can't get an "erection."

Last year *Time Magazine* featured a cover article about this subject titled "Porn: Why Young Men Who Grew Up with

Internet Porn Are Becoming Advocates for Turning It Off."[3] The article shared story after story of young men who regretted pursuing porn. Every story was similar. A guy began using porn because it was so accessible. The more he watched, the more the "same ol' thing" just wasn't stimulating. So he pursued more extreme material. Pretty soon, this young man became hooked on perfect-looking women doing everything imaginable, and his real-life sex partner wasn't enough to get the blood flowing. . .literally.

It's called impotence or erectile dysfunction (ED). Too much porn actually hinders the ability to get an erection. And the problem has only increased with the accessibility of online porn. That same *Time* article revealed how in 1992 only about 5 percent of men experienced ED at age forty (according to the US National Institutes of Health, or NIH). Fast-forward to 2013, a time when almost every home had high-speed Internet, and the *Journal of Sexual Medicine* discovered that 26 percent of men seeking help for ED were under forty. In 2014 a study of US military personnel younger than forty found that one-third were reporting ED.[4]

Bottom line: The more young men look at porn, the higher the chance of sexual dysfunction.

Many experts are calling it an addiction. Philip Zimbardo, emeritus professor of psychology at Stanford University, says, "Porn embeds you in what I call present hedonistic time zone. You seek pleasure and novelty and live for the moment."[5] He explains that while porn isn't chemically addictive, it has the same effect on behavior as a drug addiction does: Some people stop doing much else in favor of pursuing it.

But porn doesn't just affect men.

Young girls are getting the wrong message from porn. The

message is this: *You are a sex object made to fulfill the cravings of men.* And young women who visit porn sites regularly are believing the lie, along with a much more prevalent lie: *You don't look good enough.* Girls feel they need to measure up to an image that isn't even real. It's called plastic surgery, and more and more teen girls want it. The American College of Obstetricians and Gynecologists has reported a significant increase in cosmetic surgery among teen girls.[6]

The other prominent problem with porn is how it degrades women and normalizes sexual violence. Research backs up that latter fact with shocking numbers:

> *In a study of behaviors in popular porn, nearly 90 percent of 304 random scenes contained physical aggression toward women, who nearly always responded neutrally or with pleasure. More insidiously, women would sometimes beg their partners to stop, then acquiesce and begin to enjoy the activity, regardless of how painful or debasing.[7]*

Let that sink in for a moment. What is this teaching young men?

"*I know she wants it!*"

Does she?

ORIGINAL DESIGN

The whole problem with pornography is that we're not designed that way. God designed us to enjoy sex with one person to whom we commit in marriage. Sex wasn't created to share with everyone we meet. It wasn't even created for us to imagine doing it with everyone we meet.

Think about this for a moment. Do you want the person you love thinking about having sex with other people? No way.

This isn't the way it's supposed to be. Jesus even talked about this issue explicitly. He said if we even look at someone with lust, we commit adultery in our heart (Matthew 5:28). That's exactly what pornography is. It's looking at someone we aren't married to and thinking about sexual situations with them.

God knows people will regret this kind of activity. He wants the best for us, and He is sad when we try to do things our own way instead of trusting in Him.

So looking at porn doesn't just hurt us; it hurts God *and* our future spouse.

How can we avoid going down this road that leads to so much hurt, regret, and frustration? How can we avoid it specifically in a world that dangles temptation in front of us in so many forms on so many screens?

STEERING CLEAR

The Bible gives helpful advice on the subject in a letter written to a young man. I'm referring to the book of 2 Timothy. A guy named Paul shared this truth with a young man named Timothy: "Run from anything that stimulates youthful lusts. Instead, pursue righteous living, faithfulness, love, and peace. Enjoy the companionship of those who call on the Lord with pure hearts" (2 Timothy 2:22).

If you have ever been in a situation where you were tempted sexually, then you realize how incredibly relevant this verse is. In fact, this "ancient advice" (it's literally two thousand years old) might be the best advice *ever* on how to avoid being ensnared by sexual temptation over and over again.

This verse offers two excellent tips:

1. Run away. Let's be honest. We live in a world where we don't have to look very far for anything that stimulates "youthful lusts." Every device we own can access lust-inducing images within a few clicks. And that's why most of us could really benefit from following Paul's advice to run away from "anything that stimulates" this kind of thinking. It's good to know the "triggers" that stimulate lust. If you've found yourself looking at sensual images in the past, ask yourself, "How did I get into this situation?" When and where do these situations occur?

- Are you more tempted when you are home alone?
- Are you more tempted when you are looking at your mobile devices in your bedroom?
- Are these temptations encouraged by certain friends?
- Are they only on certain devices?
- Are they only within certain apps, websites, or channels?
- Do you encounter this kind of temptation more often on certain social media platforms?

As you consider these questions, ask yourself, "How can I run away from these triggers?" How can you avoid being alone or in this tempting location? Are certain people in your life leading you to make foolish decisions? Do you have some apps you might want to delete? Are there channels or websites you shouldn't visit anymore?

You might be thinking, "This sounds kind of severe!" And you're right. You're the one who has to ask yourself what it looks like to truly "run from anything that stimulates youthful lusts." (And if you think that's severe, look up what Jesus recommended to people who lusted in Matthew 5:27–30.)

Sometimes it's difficult to ask ourselves these questions about "triggers" because in all honesty, we don't like the answers. If we find ourselves getting distracted frequently on YouTube, we don't want to have to consider avoiding YouTube. We love YouTube! And it would be a sacrifice to miss all the fun stuff on YouTube just because it occasionally bombards us with sensual images.

It's pretty easy to convince ourselves that a trigger isn't really a trigger. That's probably why the verse offers this second helpful tip. . .

2. *Seek positive advisers.* The advice to "run away" is followed by the advice to "enjoy the companionship of those who call on the Lord with pure hearts." Paul doesn't want us to try to accomplish this difficult task on our own. He wants us to tackle temptation surrounded by people who will encourage us to do what's right. Paul knows "lusting" is something usually done in private. And the best way to battle something done in private is to expose it.

No, I'm not suggesting you announce your struggle in the middle of church (neither is Paul). The advice would be to find a mentor or friend who believes in God's truth and to share your struggles with this person. The Bible is full of this advice, like in Ecclesiastes 4:10 when Solomon advises, "If one person falls, the other can reach out and help."

Wouldn't it be nice to have the help of someone who can reach out and pick you up when you fall? Guys, find a godly man you trust and share your struggle. Girls, find a godly woman who can encourage you through these rough times. Surround yourself with friends you can talk to honestly about the temptations you face. God doesn't want you to go through any of these struggles alone.

QUESTIONS TO PONDER

1. Where do you think many young people first encounter sexual imagery today?
2. Do you think most young people you know feel that sexual imagery is something to avoid? Why or why not?
3. What is one of the common results of porn viewing you read about that stood out to you?
4. What does Jesus say specifically about lust? How does this relate to porn?
5. Why do you think God wants us to enjoy only one person intimately, even to the point of not "looking around" at others?
6. What is some of the advice Paul gave in 2 Timothy 2:22? How does that relate to you?
7. Is there a "trigger" you may need to remove from your life? (An app you need to delete, a device you need to remove from your bedroom, a channel you need to tell your parents to block?)
8. What is one thing you can do this week to escape the shackles of pornography?

SOMETHING TO THINK ABOUT

The world isn't completely void of good. Your phone and the Internet offer some respectable resources and tools that can be quite helpful in daily life. Stats vary, but most reveal that only 4 percent of the web is sexually explicit in nature.[8] That leaves you a lot of space to browse that won't lead you down a path you'll regret.

But if you find yourself constantly wandering down an unhealthy path, remember Paul's advice to young Timothy.

Run away! If you don't know how to do this, XXXChurch
.com has some great tools for students and parents getting
help for porn addiction.

And don't make this journey alone. Ask someone to keep
you accountable for every image you see. Give them permission to ask tough questions, such as, "Is there anything you
regret looking at this week?"

This principle of seeking out a mentor is so important, I
want to spend the entire next chapter on it.

FOR FURTHER READING

If you'd like to know more about what the Bible says about
sex and how you can realistically avoid many of these temptations, take a peek at my book *Sex Matters*.[9] Not only do I talk
about God's perfect design for sex in marriage, but I spend an
entire chapter on porn and fleeing temptation.

Tip #5

Don't do this alone.
Seeking out a mentor

*H*ave you ever heard an actor giving an Oscar acceptance speech? How about an athlete thanking everyone who ever helped them on their journey toward MVP?

It's always interesting to hear people who've made major accomplishments thank those who gave encouragement and guidance along the way.

A few years ago one of the NBA's greatest players, Allen Iverson, was inducted into the Hall of Fame. In his emotional and humorous speech, he thanked God for loving him and blessing him; he thanked Tupac and Michael Jackson for providing his theme music throughout his career; and in one of the most tender moments of his speech, he thanked Philadelphia 76ers coach Larry Brown.

> *I was an all right basketball player, I had talent. But once I started to listen to Larry Brown and take constructive criticism, I learned how much of a great, great, great coach that he is. Once I started to listen to him and was coached by him, that's when I became an MVP, I became an All-Star. . .and I followed his lead all the way.*[1]

Behind every successful person is a mentor who helped them along the journey.

- Talk show host Oprah Winfrey was mentored by Mrs. Duncan, her fourth-grade teacher.
- Dr. Martin Luther King Jr. was mentored by Benjamin E. Mays.
- Poet Henry David Thoreau was mentored by Ralph Waldo Emerson.
- Music industry legend Quincy Jones was mentored by Ray Charles.
- The late actor Heath Ledger was mentored by Mel Gibson.
- Painter Vincent van Gogh was mentored by Paul Gauguin.
- Singer and actor Frank Sinatra was mentored by Bing Crosby.
- Former Apple CEO, the late Steve Jobs, was mentored by Robert Friedland.
- Facebook's creator Mark Zuckerberg was mentored by Steve Jobs.
- Astronaut and former US senator John Glenn was mentored by his high school civics teacher.
- Actor and director Clint Eastwood was mentored by his grandmother.[2]

The list is endless—amazing people who not only survived but thrived because someone helped them through the ups and downs life handed them.

In the Bible we find many examples of mentors: Jethro mentoring Moses; Moses mentoring Joshua; Eli mentoring Samuel; Elijah mentoring Elisha; Jesus mentoring the disciples; and Paul mentoring Timothy. Paul actually mentored many leaders in various churches across the land. He urged the church in Philippi, for example, to "keep putting into practice all you learned and received from me" (Philippians 4:9).

My point is simple: Seek out a mentor! We've talked about some challenging struggles in the pages of this book already, important decisions to navigate, powerful distractions to avoid, all related to our various tech devices. Many of the choices we make on these devices in the next few years will follow us for years to come. So my advice is simple: *Don't do this alone!*

SOMEONE IN YOUR CORNER

Who is someone you can talk to about new digital landscapes?

If you have a phone in your pocket, then you know many of these decisions aren't easy. You have hundreds of apps to choose from, some of them much safer or wiser to navigate than others. You have friends stirring up drama, and you'd probably prefer not to get all caught up in the crazy. You've probably even encountered some images and content that you know you should steer away from. . .but countless voices are telling you, "It's no big deal."

It's okay to ask someone for advice about these kinds of decisions. Doing so actually shows great humility and teachability, which are the two main traits I look for when I hire someone. Most CEOs and leaders agree.

Seek out a mentor.

What great athletes do you know who don't have coaches? Seriously. . .name one!

You can't. Because they don't exist.

Think of the phrase "someone in your corner." That's a boxing term. Every great boxer has a coach in his "corner" encouraging him and giving him counsel between each round. We need someone in our corner.

This principle goes beyond athletes. Name an actor, singer, or musician who doesn't have a teacher, coach, or some kind of mentor helping them perfect their gift. Good luck finding one.

Successful people seek out mentors to help them along the way.

Mentoring expert Drew Appleby, PhD, professor emeritus at Indiana University–Purdue University Indianapolis, says it like this: "Mentors help people determine who they want to become, how they must change in order to become these people, and how they can take advantage of their college or work experiences to bring about these changes."[3]

Who is helping you become who you want to be?

Seek out a positive adult mentor to help you navigate the digital landscape. Mom and Dad are great people to help you along this path, but I'd also encourage you to seek out additional adult mentors in your life. Research reveals that most successful people have had four to five mentors in their lives who offered not only encouragement but also candid advice.

CHOOSING A MENTOR

Here are some tips to help you choose a mentor:

1. *Same faith.* If your faith is important to you, then I encourage you to find a mentor who has your same faith and values. It's this foundation from which you will make most decisions. So choose this person carefully. Your parents might be able to help you with some good possibilities. Consider a pastor, youth leader, or one of your parents' family friends whose lifestyle reveals God's undeniable influence in his or her life.

2. *Same gender.* If you're a guy, ask a man you respect. If you're a girl, ask a woman you respect. A mentor of the same gender will better understand you and coach you. Don't get me wrong; it's great to have caring men *and* women as role models in your life. I can recall several of my friends' moms who provided great wisdom and counsel to me as a young man. But when it comes to choosing a mentor you can meet with consistently, selecting a person of the same gender is far more prudent and practical.

3. *Someone who models leadership qualities you desire.* Who is someone you and your parents really respect? Don't just look for someone who seems cool. Seek out someone who shows wisdom and understanding. Choose someone who will stretch you to grow in your faith, wisdom, and interpersonal relationships.

Once you clear the person with your parents (if you're still young and living at home, it's always a good idea to keep Mom and Dad in the loop), simply ask this potential mentor, "Can you do coffee sometime this week? I need some advice." When you meet with them, tell them a little about what you're going through. Share some of the struggles you're having. If you desire some structure for your conversation, take a book like this one and ask if you can read it and discuss it with them. (That's why I've included discussion questions near the end of each chapter.)

When your first meeting comes to a close, simply ask, "Can we do this again?"

Try scheduling a time to meet regularly. Tuesday afternoons, for example. If weekly doesn't work, make it randomly ongoing. Text them one or two times a month and try to connect.

If your first attempt getting a mentor doesn't work out, don't give up. Try someone else. You'll be glad you did.

QUESTIONS TO PONDER

1. Why do people winning awards always feel compelled to thank people who helped them along the way?
2. Which adults in your life have been influential to you so far?
3. Drew Appleby said, "Mentors help people determine who they want to become, how they must change in order to become these people." What do you think are the benefits of having someone else help us "change" for the better?
4. What is one area a mentor might help you "change"?
5. Who is someone you admire for their faith, their wisdom, and the way they handle others?
6. What actions can you take this week to seek out a mentoring relationship with this person or someone similar?

SOMETHING TO THINK ABOUT

Our society has made a huge mistake in the last few decades. Somewhere between the industrial revolution and the invention of Mario Kart, we created "the kid table."

I don't know about your family, but whenever my parents held large gatherings for holidays or other celebrations, two tables were set: the grown-up table and the kid table. All the adults would hang around the grown-up table and talk about life, responsibility, bills. . .and sometimes even politics.

Meanwhile, over at the kid table, young'uns would flick peas at each other, talk about their favorite video games, and sneak seconds of dessert when the adults were engrossed in their conversation. I've seen this in homes across the country.

Churches followed suit. When families pulled into the parking lot on a Sunday morning, young people went one way and parents went the other. Teens went to "youth service" while Mom and Dad went to "big church." Sometimes the two groups would attend the same service, but even then, the teens would all sit together in one section.

Only one problem: At what age are young people ever going to experience adult conversation?

College?

Their twenties?

At what age do you get to start talking about stuff that matters with people who've actually been there?

If you've ever experienced this division, I have a piece of advice for you: Don't sit at the kid table. In fact, if you ever see this happening to younger siblings or little cousins—please intervene. That's right. I'm asking you to rebel. Demand integration. Claim a seat at the grown-up table. Furthermore, if the grown-ups are boring you with their conversation, then change the conversation to a topic you want. It's simple. Just ask questions.

- Did you ever play video games when you were a kid?
- What were they like?
- Tell me when you knew Mom was "the one."
- If you had life to do over again, what's one thing you would do differently?

- If you could go back and give one piece of advice to "you" in high school, what would you tell yourself?

Believe it or not, you can learn a lot from the adults in the room. . .and they most likely can learn something from you.

Tip #6

Unmask.
The myth of anonymity

I'll never forget the poignant scene from the Oscar-winning film *Places in the Heart* when the KKK showed up at the old farmhouse in an attempt to lynch Moze, a likable farmhand played by actor Danny Glover. The old white men, masquerading in their emblematic white pillowcase hoods, began beating Moze, whose only trespass was the dark color of his skin. But then Mr. Will walked out, and everything changed.

Mr. Will was blind. He was born blind and had spent a lifetime adapting to his other senses.

The hooded men continued beating Moze, boldly yelling at Mr. Will to go back into the farmhouse and mind his own business.

Recognizing the men's voices, Mr. Will identified each assailant as he spoke. *"Mr. Simmons. Mr. Thompson. Mr. Shaw."*

The men froze, silenced as they heard their names called out. Their white hoods no longer served any purpose.

Their anonymity had been stripped away.

One by one they retreated, frightened by one element: accountability.

Sadly, many people would love the absence of accountability. As much as we might wish we were not responsible for our actions, our accountability is an unavoidable truth. Some cultures call it karma—"What goes around comes around." In other words, accountability involves accepting the natural consequences of our behavior.

Some of us have experienced moments when any sense of accountability has been removed. Locker room talk when the coach is away. Secretive whispers when the teacher can't hear. The fabricated sense of recklessness or irresponsibility when Mom leaves us home by ourselves for a few hours.

Why do we enjoy this feeling so much?

Part of it is natural. As we grow older, our biological instinct is to become more independent. Believe it or not, Mom and Dad actually *want* you to become more independent. They hope you won't still be living in their basement when you're thirty-five years old. But when you're thirteen or even fifteen years old, the desire to be independent sometimes reveals itself as "I don't need Mom and Dad!" or "My teachers don't know what's best for me!" or even "I know what I'm doing and I don't need any help." This is why it's common for young people to seek out places where they can just be themselves, places where they can express themselves without criticism or repercussion. I totally understand the desire to express yourself without being analyzed or corrected at every turn.

I assure you, your parents sought out moments of independence and venues without adult supervision when they were your age. For them, it was hanging out at the mall or maybe the drive-in with their friends. But fast-forward to present-day and consider where this desire for independence has steered us as a culture of constantly connected device owners. Now young people often seek out independence in the online world. Hence the growing trend of something called "ephemeral anonymity."

GETTING AWAY WITH IT

Ephemeral is just a word that means "short-lived" or in existence for only a short time. Ephemeral apps provide the perception that what you type or post will be there for only a short time. Snapchat is the perfect example of a perceived ephemeral app. The pictures disappear, right? (I'll devote an entire chapter to this soon.)

Anonymity is the state of being unidentified, unrecognized, or anonymous. Maybe you're only an unrecognized username in a comment section of a YouTube video. The video is of an underconfident blond teenage girl in her room singing into a hairbrush as if it were a microphone. Since your username is just Dski247, you feel the anonymity and freedom to type, "I'd rather listen to a dying cat, you fat snowbeast!"

Sound mean? Sadly, it just sounds typical if you read comments in today's social media. People can be brutal!

Many young people today seek out online settings where they can anonymously post words or pictures that not only aren't connected to their true identity but also disappear. Experts call it *ephemeral anonymity*. And young people love it.

Why?

Anonymously posting disappearing content on social media allows us to avoid both personal responsibility and public scrutiny for our actions. It gives us the feeling that we can get away with whatever we want.

There are two problems with this idea:

1. Ephemeral anonymity provides a false sense of security. Earlier in this book we learned that nothing we post on the Internet is truly temporary or anonymous. People are always surprised when they discover their

"private" conversations weren't actually private. Anonymous apps like Whisper and Secret both claimed to be anonymous apps. One of them even claimed to be "the safest place on the Internet." But both struggled to deliver on that claim.[1] In fact, journalists at the *Guardian* discovered that Whisper not only tracked the locations of users but stored posts for literally years, when they claimed their policy was to hold on to data for only "a brief period of time."[2] (Maybe they thought "years" was brief?) Snapchat underwent a similar investigation (again, more on that later). Bottom line: People who wish for a private place to talk where their words will never come back to haunt them *rarely find such a place.*

2. This perceived lack of accountability always cultivates bad decision-making. When people think they can get away with something, they tend to do stupid things. . .and not get away with it.

What does this mean for you?

Anonymity is actually only perceived anonymity, and it breeds carelessness. Like the seventeen-year-old student from Michigan who posted on the anonymous app After School: *"Id rather take my AR 15 to school and practice on my classmates than to the gun range."*

The comment proved not to be as anonymous as he thought because he was arrested, pleaded guilty to using a computer in a crime and making a terrorist threat, and was sentenced to ninety days in jail.[3]

I wonder what this seventeen-year-old would say to Cory Levy, the twenty-four-year-old founder of After School who claimed the app gives teens a chance to "express themselves without worrying about any backlash or any repercussions."

I guess that doesn't include jail time.

The world is embracing anonymity because people desire a lack of accountability.[4] But the truth is, we are all accountable for our actions and our comments. Our words matter.

Consider the words of Peter in the Bible:

> *If anyone speaks, they should do so as one who speaks the very words of God. If anyone serves, they should do so with the strength God provides, so that in all things God may be praised through Jesus Christ. To him be the glory and the power for ever and ever. Amen.* (1 Peter 4:11 NIV)

Peter asks us to consider our words carefully, as though God Himself were speaking through us. He advises us to do the same with our actions. Imagine how the comments on social media would change if people were following that advice.

Sadly, many people are doing the exact opposite of that instruction. They are literally trying to hide behind the guise of anonymity because they know their words are shameful.

It's the same principle we discussed earlier in the book about people wanting their posts to disappear. When people engage in bad behaviors, they don't typically like to do it in the light.

Maybe we should just avoid those kinds of behaviors—then we won't need to hide.

QUESTIONS TO PONDER

1. Why do people feel more confident to act cruelly or carelessly when they are anonymous?

2. What are healthy ways young people can practice their independence?
3. What have you noticed from people in anonymous settings like the comment section of websites?
4. Do your words actually matter? Explain.
5. In 1 Peter 4:11, how does Peter say we should speak? What does that mean?
6. What does the verse mean when it says, ". . .so that in all things God may be praised through Jesus Christ"?
7. How can our words and actions reflect Christ?
8. What might it look like in your life to consider what God wants you to say or do before saying or doing it? What is one way you can live that out this week?

SOMETHING TO THINK ABOUT

Some young people have become fed up with the online cruelty that is so common in anonymous apps. In fact, a group of students began petitioning the app After School, one posting:

"With the shield of anonymity, users have zero accountability for their posts, and can openly spread rumors, call classmates hurtful names, send threats, or even tell someone to kill themselves—and all of these things are happening."[5]

Apple pulled the app from its store that same month, forcing the app to revamp many of its safety features, including a quick response system where authorities could be contacted if danger or threats were detected.

Anonymous apps give people a sense of security and a seeming lack of accountability, when in fact *they provide neither*. Sadly, this isn't their only weakness. They also tend to make you feel safe talking to people you've never met in person.

Is this a big deal?

Let's spend some time talking about that in the next chapter.

Tip #7

Yes, still don't talk with strangers.
Do you really know who you're hanging out with?

Thirteen-year-old Nicole met him on Kik, a social media app known for shielding people's identity. The two chatted for months. As time passed, the conversations became a little more intimate. Eventually, the stranger, who later was identified as a college student from Virginia Tech, lured her out of her house to meet. Three days later she was found dead 100 miles from her home.[1]

Nicole liked meeting new people on social media. She had a history of talking with guys she met on these sites. Many were older guys posing as younger guys. Her sister and her parents both warned her about her online activity. Her parents even took her phone away. It was returned shortly before her disappearance.

She heard the warnings. She just never thought she was in danger.

NOT ME

Most of us seem to have an inner wiring that tells us, "It won't happen to me." We figure safety protocols are just out there to scare us. These things don't really happen. . .do they?

I talk to teenagers about this subject in school assemblies across the US. Most listen, and many find my talks informative. But countless teenagers will tell me to my face, "It won't happen to me."

Sadly, I also spend countless hours with principals, coaches, teachers, and parents. . .all who tell me stories of their kids ignoring safety protocols, bypassing privacy settings, and letting down their guard on social media. The examples are endless. Like the Maryland teenager who met a guy on social media—on an app that actually brags "Meet new people." She was so convinced this guy was nice, she revealed her true identity and decided to meet him in person. The police found her body later that evening in Washington, DC.[2]

Most of these stories have common denominators: young people talking with strangers on social media. Over time, most reveal their identity or their location. The stories rarely have good endings.

Fortunately, many of these strangers are caught. Like the twenty-three-year-old who was arrested shortly after jumping out the window of a twelve-year-old's bedroom when Mom and Dad walked in.[3] Thankfully, this guy is in jail facing charges of lewd acts on a minor under fourteen years old. Sadly, this girl's life will never be the same.

Or consider the girl from Nebraska who met a man online and, after a few weeks of correspondence, agreed to meet with him. They met, and he took her back to a house where he sexually assaulted her. Luckily she lived to tell the tale. Although I doubt she would ever use the word *lucky* to describe her situation.[4]

And not only girls are in danger. A Southern California man was just arrested for luring male juveniles he met on social media, committing "lewd sexual acts" with them, and then distributing child pornography.[5]

If you want to see exactly how common this kind of activity is, just Google the words "man arrested met on social media" and you'll have reading material for days.

The creepers are so common, many towns have an entire special investigations unit in their police department dedicated to these online predators. After one of my workshops in New Jersey, I was talking with a sixteen-year-old girl and her mother. This teenager didn't have her phone anymore. The police had it. They were hoping the guy she had been chatting with would try to contact her again so they could lure him to a meeting place and capture him.

They didn't have any information about him other than the picture he sent. . .and it wasn't of his face.

"It happens all the time," the special investigator told them. "Young people meet someone on social media, they give out their phone number or address, and it isn't long before they realize the person they were talking to isn't the person they thought they were talking to."

I hear stories like this from parents, teachers, and coaches all too frequently. Most often it sounds something like this:

1. Girl meets boy online—"He was really sweet."
2. Eventually, sometimes weeks or even months later, boy asks girl for some personal information, often something that might sound harmless—"What school do you go to?"
3. Boy discovers girl's real identity.
4. Boy sends pics.
5. Boy asks girl to send pics—"Come on, I sent one. It's your turn."
6. Boy asks to meet.

Most girls don't randomly meet with some stranger who says,

"Let's meet," on day one. The good predators are patient. In fact, the good predators are working a dozen people at once all on different time frames.

How common is this sort of situation?

It's more common than you think in a world where 57 percent of thirteen- to seventeen-year-olds have met a new friend online.[6] The most common way these teens meet new people online is through social media and online game-play. In the majority of these situations the young person has absolutely no idea who they are talking with on the other end of the connection.

A FALSE SENSE OF SECURITY

Remember when your mom told you, "Don't talk with strangers"?

That's good advice.

Seriously. A screen doesn't change things much. . .except maybe that screens can be even *more* dangerous because of all the information they provide.

Think about it. If you stop at a grocery store and talk with a stranger, you actually might be safer than when you chat with someone online. Why?

- In a grocery store you are surrounded by people.
- In a grocery store the person can't click on your profile and see if you accidentally posted something about where you live or go to school. And they can't see the pictures you posted last weekend with all your friends.
- In a grocery store the person isn't hidden behind the guise of a username and fake picture concealing their identity. You have a pretty good idea if you're talking

to a teenager or an adult, a man or a woman, someone with clothes on or. . .

Please don't get me wrong. I'm not trying to convince you to start sharing personal information with people in grocery stores based on their outer appearance. I'm just trying to help you realize that online relationships provide more "unknowns" than "knowns." So be careful what you share online. Be careful to use your privacy settings (we already spent a chapter talking about that). Think before you post: *Is there any way this picture or post gives away too much about my identity or my location?*

WHAT IF THEY AREN'T A PREDATOR?

Yes, social media is also filled with people who actually aren't pedophiles. Many of them are young people looking for relationships. . .or hookups.

So forget those creepy predators for a second. Let's consider that it really is just a boy who wants a girl to send him a sensual picture.

Girls, is this really the kind of guy you want? Ask someone older than you who has been there. Better yet, ask ten women you respect. Ask them, "If a guy is asking me to share private information, talk sensually, or even send sexy pics, could this be a nice guy?"

I promise you, ten out of ten women will tell you, "Run away!"

And guys, if you meet a girl online who is talking erotically, how will that end? Honestly, think it through. Maybe you're stimulated while talking with her. What then? Are you going to meet this girl? And even if she isn't a forty-seven-year-old man posing as a girl, but a real girl, is this really the kind of girl you want? Do you want a relationship with her? If so, will she stop going online and talking about sex with other guys?

No matter how you play it out, it doesn't end well.

Let me propose something that can save you a world of pain, frustration, and embarrassment: Don't chat with someone you haven't met face-to-face. You don't want to get caught up in all that crazy.

RED FLAGS

Some young people won't heed that advice. They'll opt to get caught up in the crazy. Or maybe they're just gamers who like playing with people online and don't see the danger.

If you feel like you *must* talk with people online, then keep your eyes open for words, phrases, or questions that are commonly used by online predators. I call these "red flags" because when you see them, they should be like a red flag waving in your face and screaming, "Creeper!"

The most obvious red flag is if they ask for your name, address, or phone number. You don't need to give those out—*ever*. But sometimes they're subtler.

- "Are you a girl or a guy?"
- "What are you wearing?"
- "What school do you go to?"
- "What mall do you usually shop at?"
- "I know that area—what neighborhood do you live in?"
- Any invasive or sexual questions
- Anything that makes you *feel* uncomfortable

Also be on the lookout for "catfish." A catfish is anyone who creates a false identity online so they can steal from you or lure you into a romantic relationship. Look for any of these tell-tale signs:

- They won't ever Facetime or video-chat with you. And even if they say they will, something always comes up when it's time to chat.
- They get serious in a short period of time. If someone is pushing the relationship forward, claiming they "fell for you" after just a few conversations, there's a good chance you're dealing with a catfish.
- They mention modeling or being famous. Catfish often claim to have careers that impress people by title alone or hint that the person must be good-looking.
- They ask you for money. Catfish never seem to have any other friends or family to get money from.
- They travel out of the country a lot. International travel gives them an excuse for odd hours or behaviors. Many catfish claim to travel abroad for work.
- They can't meet you or your family in person. Again, I don't recommend talking with strangers, and I certainly don't recommend meeting them in person. But if you are someone who insists on doing so, and you choose a public place just to be safe, a catfish will always have some excuse why they can't meet. Sometimes they'll use tragedy as an excuse. "My mom was just in a car wreck." "My grandma was just diagnosed with cancer." Because who's going to press someone about that?
- They don't have any real friends or pictures with their friends in their Facebook profile. Most real people have pictures with friends and then tag those friends

in their social media profiles. If this person doesn't tag friends, there's a good chance this person has robbed someone else's pictures and is using them.

But catfish aren't the only dangerous people you could meet online, and some shady people won't necessarily try to get money *from* you. Sometimes online "friends" might ask for your phone number or address so they can *send you* something. A mom contacted me when I was in the middle of writing this book and asked me for advice. Her teenage son "Jake" met some online friends while gaming. Jake didn't have a very good gaming system, and one of these friends offered to help him upgrade his system. "I've got plenty of money," this new friend claimed. "My family is in the oil industry." Excited about the possibility of upgrading his system, Jake gave his home address to this anonymous nineteen-year-old friend. A few days later a package arrived containing several Christmas gifts and a large amount of cash. His mom asked me what to do, and I advised them to call the police. Sure enough, this friend whose family was supposedly "in the oil industry" shipped the package from a trailer park, a location where a forty-year-old of the same name was registered as a sex offender. As I write this, a detective who specializes in Internet child solicitation is taking over to expose the true identity of this anonymous "friend."

I can't warn you enough. This stuff happens *all the time*!

Watch out for people seeking to get to know you in gaming or chat-room settings. Be careful who you communicate with and surround yourself with.

Don't take it from me; take it from the Word of God. The apostle Paul shared a relevant truth long ago that is just as applicable today. He was warning his readers about some bad people and advised, "Do not be misled: 'Bad company corrupts good character'" (1 Corinthians 15:33 NIV). In fact, when he said this, he was actually quoting a Greek poet of his day, a guy named Menander. It was a common saying, because even back then it was a well-known fact that if you surround yourself with bad people, their dirt always rubs off on you.

The problem is, it's hard to know what's gonna rub off on us if we don't even know who we're hanging out with.

QUESTIONS TO PONDER

1. Why do you think so many people enjoy talking with strangers online?
2. Have you ever encountered creepy people online? What happened?
3. Why do so many teenagers think nothing bad will ever happen to them? Why do you think so many young people are blind to predators?
4. Is there a possibility you are overconfident about your immunity to online predators? Explain.
5. What did Paul mean by "Bad company corrupts good character"?
6. What does that look like in the online world?
7. What does that look like in your world?
8. What is one online habit you might need to adjust this week?

SOMETHING TO THINK ABOUT

Sydney met a guy on the Kik app, and the two began messaging back and forth. Sydney was just fourteen years old. Many of her relationships at school were in turmoil, so she turned to social media for comfort. The anonymity gave her a feeling of safety.

As the two of them talked, the conversation grew personal. She eventually shared deep secrets, things she had never shared with anyone else.

The stranger began talking with her about "erotic asphyxiation," or breath control play, which is the intentional restriction of oxygen to the brain for the purposes of sexual arousal. This guy talked Sydney into trying it and literally guided her step by step. Sydney retrieved one of her belts, placed it around her neck, and followed his instructions. Her mom found her dead with the belt around her neck hours later.[7]

True story. It happened in Alabama just over a year ago, as I write this.

Do you think Sydney thought she was in any danger?

Who are you having conversations with?

Tip #8

Take more "selflessies."
Recognizing when selfies become too "selfy"

He flexes in the mirror, looking up from his phone in an attempt to look hot for the camera.

Click.

He studies the picture. *Hmm. Abs don't look prominent enough.* He shifts his body and tries again.

Across the country a young girl the same age, same grade, using the same app holds her phone up at a high angle and strikes a sexy pose.

Click.

She inspects the picture. *Nope. Too much arm fat.* She takes another pic.

After four tries she captures the image she wants. *Now to apply filters. . .*

Eleven minutes later the picture is posted.

Funny. . .less than a decade ago no one even knew what a selfie was. Now young people average nine selfies per week, spending an average of seven minutes perfecting each one before posting. That adds up to about fifty-four hours per year of selfies.[1]

What were we doing with those fifty-four hours just a few years ago?

A selfie, by most people's definition, is a picture of yourself including your face, taken by yourself and posted on social media. A picture of five friends crammed into a Taco Bell booth is not a selfie. A picture of your cat asleep on the roof of your Hyundai is not a selfie. A picture of yourself trying to be sexy in your pj's through a bathroom mirror with the caption "Look how dirty this mirror is". . .*is a selfie*! (And a little pathetic.)

Sometimes the media gives the concept of selfies a bad rap. Maybe because some think selfies are a little "selfy." Think about it. Some selfies seem to scream, *Look at me. Check me out. Do you "like" me?*

Don't get me wrong. Selfies can be fun. We climb a mountain; we visit a friend and want to record the occasion; we share something enjoyable—*I bet you wish you were drinking this milk shake right now!* Posting an occasional selfie serves as a diary of sorts. But let me ask you honestly: How much "self" is too much?

My daughters were hanging out with a bunch of their friends at our house, laughing as they stared at their phones.

I couldn't help but ask, "What's so funny?"

One of the girls replied, "It's better if I just show you."

She showed me a post where a teenager wrote a lengthy discourse about a beautiful sunset. I read the text first. "I'm here admiring this amazing sky. Wish you could see it. So gorgeous!" He went on and on for a paragraph.

I scrolled up and looked at the picture. His face took up over 90 percent of the frame. In the top left corner you could barely see a speck of pretty sky. . .behind his huge cranium!

The girls all burst out laughing. One of the girls yelled at her phone, "Move your big ol' head!"

You've probably heard the term "self-absorbed."

Maybe some of us should consider whether we are "selfie-absorbed."

WHEN SELFIES BECOME TOO "SELFY"

Watch for the following warning signs:

1. You're so busy documenting the moment, you miss the moment!

Have you ever been somewhere amazing with your friends, like the beach or an amusement park, and they're so buried in their phones that they're missing all the fun? And then when you confront them, they say, "Almost finished. I'm just posting something."

Meanwhile, a hawk swoops down and carries off a Chihuahua right in front of your eyes. . .and they miss it because they were posting a picture of their freshly painted toenails.

We could try to just point our finger at our friends, but the truth is, many of us probably find ourselves doing this, too.

Don't get so caught up in posting the moment that you miss the moment.

Don't worry—you're not alone in this. Sometimes even Mom or Dad will succumb to this temptation. They'll take a picture of you during your soccer game, and while they're spending nine minutes posting it for all their friends to see, they miss seeing you make a goal (or seeing you get whopped in the face with the ball, which is much more picturesque, don't you think?).

So put down your phone every once in a while and enjoy your surroundings the good old-fashioned way. Laugh at two seagulls fighting over a bag of chips. Soak in the beauty of the snowcapped mountains. Close your eyes and feel the wind blowing gently through your hair. And if you absolutely have to post something, then grab one quick pic that truly represents the moment. Maybe even post it later when you're bored out of your mind during the car ride home or in your bedroom. Just don't miss the moment.

2. Your pictures don't even look like you.

We've all seen hilarious selfies where people have altered the picture to make themselves thinner, more muscular, more sun-bronzed. . .you name it. You might have even had the experience of meeting a friend-of-a-friend for the first time face-to-face—someone you'd only seen pictures of—and finding they look *nothing* like their pictures!

If this is you, you might want to ease off the filters or the Photoshop just a bit. Many people struggle with insecurities and have trouble finding pics that make them feel good about themselves (we'll talk more about this struggle in the next chapter), but altering a pic is not an option. This isn't *Jurassic Park*. You don't shoot and then add the digital effects later (even if you feel like a brontosaurus).

Your real friends want to see the real you!

3. Too much you.

Even if you're really cute, we only want to see so much *you*. Don't take too many selfies. It comes across as "selfy." Online magazine *The Week* claims, "Selfies are like paychecks. You only get two a month."[2] *Vogue*'s article "The Instagram Rules: The Good, the Bad, and the Very Boring" recommends never taking a selfie unless you absolutely have to.[3] So minimize your selfies. It's better to take pictures of your dog wearing the cone of shame, your sister's baby playing the piano naked. . .your dad's hamburger with four patties!

4. You're all about the likes!

How many likes are enough? Ten? Twenty? Fifty?

If you find yourself checking likes each day, seeking some sort of social media validation, then you might want to re-evaluate social media altogether. This isn't reality TV. You don't need votes to survive. (We'll talk more about this issue later in the book.)

Do you relate to any of these four warning signs? If so, you might want to consider posting more "selflessies" than selfies. Instead of taking yet another picture of your own face, take a picture of your friend or of their science project, their bedazzled coffee mug, their skateboard—anything they value—and say something nice about it.

Let me ask you this: Which friends do you prefer to be around—the ones who talk about themselves all the time, or the ones who pay attention to you and listen to you when you need them?

Self-absorbed people aren't fun to be around. Who wants to hang out with people who are so focused on themselves that they actually overlook the needs of the people around them?

Researchers call this a *lack of empathy*, and it's one of the common side effects discovered in people who spend a lot of time absorbed in social media. You probably don't need someone with a PhD to convince you of this reality—when your friends spend too much time focused on themselves, they tend not to empathize with others or to seek to understand the needs of others.

Is this the kind of person you want to hang out with?

Is this the kind of person you want to be?

Try an experiment in the next twenty-four hours. When

you get up in the morning, promise yourself that you will spend the entire day caring about the needs of others before your own needs. In other words, you won't do anything out of selfish desire; instead you will consider others better than yourself.

Here's what this might look like in your world:

- Don't grab the last piece of bread for your toast in the morning. Offer it to someone else in your family.
- Ask your mom if there is anything you can help her do before you go to school.
- Don't call "Shotgun!" on the way to school. Offer someone else the best seat.
- Compliment your teacher about something they said or taught.
- Sit by someone who typically sits by herself and ask her about her week.
- When you get home, do a chore someone else in your family hates.

Or in the world of social media:

- Post a positive comment about something someone posted.
- Post a picture of a good friend and say something kind about them.
- Post a picture of a family member and say something uplifting about them.
- Text someone about something positive you noticed about them.

I'd be lying if I told you this was my advice to you. I actually stole it from the Bible. This advice was given about two thousand years ago by the apostle Paul in his letter to the people living in the city of Philippi, located in northeastern Greece. In that letter he said, "Don't be selfish; don't try to impress others. Be humble, thinking of others as better than yourselves. Don't look out only for your own interests, but take an interest in others, too. You must have the same attitude that Christ Jesus had" (Philippians 2:3–5).

Does this advice sound familiar?

It's an expansion of "the Golden Rule" Jesus taught when He asked us to "do to others whatever you would like them to do to you." It makes sense if you think about it. The best cure for selfishness is selflessly thinking about the needs of others.

Try an experiment sometime. If you are feeling down and depressed, go volunteer at a local food bank or homeless shelter. Do you know what will happen? You'll feel better about yourself. Now don't misunderstand me. I'm not telling you to serve others just so you can feel good about yourself. (Chances are, if you serve with bad motives, you won't feel any better anyway.) I'm simply saying that caring for others and serving them broadens your worldview and puts your life in perspective. . .plus you will experience the joy of helping others.

It's a little mind-boggling to think about: When you're selfless, you feel better about yourself.

Kinda makes you want to go serve somewhere, huh? (And it's okay to snap a pic with the other workers when you're done!)

QUESTIONS TO PONDER

1. Do you agree with the studies showing that too much

social media leads to a lack of empathy or compassion for others? Explain.

2. What are the character traits of someone who is self-absorbed? What is it like to hang out with this person?

3. Now think of someone who is truly considerate of other people and looks out for others' interests before their own. Describe what it's like to hang out with this person.

4. Which of these types of people do *you* hang out with more often?

5. Which of these are you?

6. Give an example of what it might look like for you to consider others better than yourself and not look out for your own interests but the interests of others.

7. What would this look like in your world of texting, social media, or gaming?

8. What is something you can do to live out selflessness this week?

SOMETHING TO THINK ABOUT

In November 2015, an Australian teenager with more than half a million followers on Instagram quit the platform altogether, claiming it was "contrived perfection made to get attention."[4] Essena O'Neill confessed how she used to check her posts time and time again to see if anyone liked them, hungry for social media validation. Finally, after growing tired of the pressure to appear a certain way, she quit all social media to "focus on real-life projects."[5]

Social media is a lot of fun. It helps us connect with friends who aren't within arm's reach, and it even allows us to show artistic flair. But sometimes social media becomes yet another platform where we feel we have to measure up.

Relieve yourself of that pressure.

Self-absorption is a lonely path.

You have the power to make an impact in the lives of others. Put aside your own interests for a moment. How can you make others feel better about themselves today?

Tip #9

Like me!
Uncovering your true identity

Are you addicted to your "likes"?

Addicted might sound like a strong word, but researchers who study the brain are using that terminology.

They're called brain mappers. Yes, that's a real job. They are a group of researchers who want to discover what goes on in the heads of today's teenagers when they use social media. A few of these brain mappers from UCLA hooked up thirty-two teenagers to MRIs and turned them loose on a customized platform akin to Instagram, all while monitoring the different areas of the brain for activity. What they found was intriguing.

Every time a teen's picture, post, or comment was "liked," their brain lit up in the area that produces oxytocin, a hormone that makes you feel good.[1] This wasn't surprising. Research in numerous studies reveals that ongoing interaction on social media often elevates the production of both oxytocin and dopamine, "mimicking what happens when we have a drug addiction."[2]

Oxytocin and dopamine are powerful neurochemicals in our brain. In fact, dopamine is the same chemical people get hit with when eating, being sexually aroused, or doing drugs.[3] It can be addictive.

That's what researchers noticed with these thirty-two teenagers. Every time the researchers "liked" any of the posts by one of the subjects, that teen's brain would literally light up with pleasure. Accordingly, they'd attempt to create even more "likable" posts, eager to receive that dopamine hit.

Here's the problem.

Once people get used to these hits of dopamine, they want more. So they seek to get more from the same source. It's a learned behavior. If something makes us feel good, we often become "conditioned" to repeat the same actions to receive the same reward. This is nothing new. If you ever take a psychology class, you'll read about a famous experiment that a man named B. F. Skinner performed on rats. He put hungry rats in a special box he designed with a lever on one of the walls. The rats would rummage around looking for food, and when they accidentally rubbed up against the lever, a food pellet would drop out of a slot next to the lever. The rats would repeat this behavior, pushing on the lever so another pellet would drop out. Before long, the rats became conditioned to repeat the behavior simply because they liked food pellets.

Isn't it nice to be compared to rats?

Even though people are smarter than rats, we often show the same signs of what Skinner called "operant conditioning." Or as he worded it, "Behavior which is reinforced tends to be repeated."[4] We post a video of our cat chasing the vacuum cleaner, and "likes" explode across our screen. Our immediate thought is *What other crazy new video can I shoot!* After all, who doesn't want to be liked?

So we try again, and the likes begin stacking up.

Dopamine hit. Dopamine hit. Dopamine hit.

Again and again we post. But then we start to notice that some of our posts don't get liked. We begin to question our own posts.

Funny, they didn't like the video of my dog wearing my hat. Why not?

Or worse yet, we notice someone else's post that got *waaaaay* more likes than we ever get. Then the likes are never enough. It's called "Instagram envy." It's common enough that they actually have a name for it.

Why does she have more likes than me? She's so awkward!

Likes feel pretty good when they're coming in, but when they don't. . .no dopamine hit.

Sometimes people become frantic for likes. You've probably witnessed this if you've ever thumbed through the various posts on social media. We see these desperate attempts to be liked in many forms:

- The desperately sexy selfie. A picture by a young girl, from a high angle, showing a little too much. Or by the proverbial shirtless male, so eager to show off the abs he's been working on. Which is much like. . .
- The "look at me" workout pic. The pic showing muscles or lean body tissue in an eager attempt to garner "Wow! You look carved like a Michelangelo sculpture!" comments.
- The wealthie. A picture, often shot by celebs, showing off their car, their overpriced outfit, or their flashy jewelry.
- Frexting. The all-too-common occurrence where friends send sexy pics to friends seeking approval. Yeah. . .it actually happens, most often by a girl seeking approval from a close friend about her body.

All these are anxious attempts to get others to "like me." And sometimes the likes come, so we continue the behavior, attempting to please everyone with post after post, like rats hitting that lever over and over again.

But guess what?

You're not a rat.

VALUABLE

You're worth far more than the "likes" you receive.

I know, I know. The world values likes just as the world values fame, income, and looks. It's hard not to be intrigued by all these elements, especially when they are dangled all around us on every screen we look at. And to make matters more confusing, social media has created a place where all you need to do is stand out! This phenomenon is somewhat bittersweet. On one hand, it's refreshing that not only the rich and perfect-looking are becoming famous; on the other hand, people now are trying literally *anything* to become famous. Because all you need is access to a device. . .and a lot of "likes"!

But likes can be so misleading, because again, your value is determined by followers, clicks, or thumbs-up. Sure, it feels good when we get that "like." But let me ask you an honest question: When do we become a little too focused on likes?

Think about it. Does a digital thumbs-up truly determine the value of people today?

Consider the woman who works at the food bank down the street from you, selflessly giving food to hundreds of families each week. Does she need a thumbs-up to be valuable?

Consider the elderly man who now lives in a rest home. He has numerous pins on a dusty old Marine uniform hanging in his closet, from a war fought long before you were born. He laid his life on the line, not only for his country, but for one of his friends who served by his side and was able to go home to a family because of his sacrifice. Does he need likes to be valuable?

Consider the single mom working two jobs just to pay rent and put food on the table for her two boys. She doesn't even have time for social media, and frankly, she'd rather spend time with her boys than social media. Is she not valuable?

Are these people less valuable than the girl with the perfectly lined lips who has over twenty thousand Insta followers?

Likes don't determine your value.

It's true. Just because Kanye West has more likes than you doesn't mean he's more liked! (Seriously. . .he's not!)

Likes often reflect *popularity*. Popularity doesn't equal value. Remember, even Hitler was popular, but that doesn't mean he was truly liked.

THE HEART

Let me ask you an important question: What's more valuable—your outward appearance or who you are inside?

The world has been getting this one messed up for literally thousands of years, even way back in Bible times when Israel was searching for a godly king. You may have heard the story. It's in the book of 1 Samuel, chapter 16. In short, God tells Samuel to go to the home of a man named Jesse and anoint one of his sons as king. God says, "I will show you which of his sons to anoint for me" (1 Samuel 16:3). When Samuel showed up, Jesse brought in his sons for Samuel. The oldest, Eliab, was noticeably tall and muscular. His abs had abs. If this guy had Instagram, he would have had thousands of followers!

Samuel took one look at Eliab and thought, *This is definitely the one God will anoint as king!*

But God had other plans. In fact, in verse 7 we read, "But the LORD said to Samuel, 'Don't judge by his appearance or height, for I have rejected him. The LORD doesn't see things the way you see them. People judge by outward appearance, but the LORD looks at the heart.'"

Jesse showed Samuel more of his sons. But God rejected each one of them. Finally Samuel asked, "Are these all the sons you have?" Sure enough, Jesse had one other son out watching the sheep and goats. He was the youngest and the smallest.

In that culture, *young* and *small* weren't valued at all. And shepherds were valued even less. (Worst job ever!)

The firstborn, however, was of the utmost value. The tallest and strongest was valued. Little kids watching sheep had the least amount of "likes" in the bunch.

But when Jesse brought his youngest son, David, before Samuel, God said, "This is the one. Anoint him as king."

QUESTIONS TO PONDER

1. Why do you think people post so many pictures of themselves today? Is it just an expression of creativity or a way of documenting the moment. . .or could it be an effort to receive validation? (Or a mix of some of these?)
2. Have you ever posted something that received a lot of likes? How did that make you feel?
3. Be honest: Have you ever been disappointed by a lack of likes?
4. What do you see valued or "liked" the most in the world of social media?
5. Why did Samuel value Eliab the most?
6. According to verse 7, how do people judge others? Give an example of how that's true today.
7. According to the same verse, how does God judge

people? What does that mean?

8. Why does God care more about who we are inside?

9. How can you develop who you are on the inside?

SOMETHING TO THINK ABOUT

I'll be honest. I have to limit my social media time because of this "like me" struggle.

That might sound a little weird. Why does a forty-something-year-old dad with a loving wife struggle with self-esteem?

It's simple: jealousy, mixed with my own feelings of inadequacy.

I typically open Instagram to see what my real-life friends are posting or to laugh at some of the funny people I follow. But it happens almost anytime I open it. I see other people doing amazing things and part of me says, *I wish I could be doing that.*

Apparently I'm not alone. A recent study showed that among nineteen- to thirty-two year olds, those who checked social media most often in the group were more than twice as likely to show signs of depression as others who checked social media in moderate amounts.[5]

Social media has a tendency to make us feel inadequate. I recognize this, I realize I struggle with this. . .so I limit my social media time.

I also make sure I'm getting a steady dose of truth in my life, and that comes from God's Word. I've found the more time I spend absorbing God's truth from the Bible, the less I believe the lies that make me feel bad about myself, lies that tell me I'm not good-looking enough, tall enough, slim enough, muscular enough, or creative enough. God's Word reminds me that it's not outward appearance but my heart that matters.

Today I actually prayed a prayer written by King David. . . the same David who was once a small young shepherd boy. He prayed, "Create in me a clean heart, O God. Renew a loyal spirit within me" (Psalm 51:10).

In a world that focuses so much on "likes" and outward appearances, try praying that God will change you from the inside out.

Tip #10

Know the app before you snap.
Exploring the intricacies of Snapchat

*B*usiness Insider calls Snapchat "the favorite communication app used by young people today. . .by a landslide."[1]

It's no surprise. It's like texting but intertwined with spontaneous pics and fun filters. It's an easy way to express yourself.

- *"So much homework!"* —sent with a picture of your laptop open next to a stack of books
- *"Morning coffee run!"* —sent with a picture of your favorite Starbucks mug
- *"Jealous!!!"* —sent with a selfie, jaw dropped, in response to your friend's snap of the ginormous cinnamon roll she was eating

Waaaaay more fun than texting!

Snapchat probably needs no introduction. It's the app that allows users to take a picture or video, type about forty characters, and then send it to whomever they choose. . .but then the content "disappears" seconds after being viewed.

Kind of.

And that's where many people fall short in their understanding of Snapchat. Sure, it's fun, and almost everyone seems to be using it, but it would be wise to know the app before you snap.

Let's look at two important facts about Snapchat and the people who created it.

1. Snapchat was created as "the best way to sext."

I know, I know. But you don't use it for sending nudes. You just use it like texting, but with your beautiful face. Maybe so, but that wasn't the original intention.

The app began when a Stanford student walked into his friend's dorm room and expressed regret over a picture he had sent and basically suggested, "I wish there was an app to send disappearing photos."

The two pondered the idea for a moment.

Send whatever you want, but with no consequences.

One thing led to another, and these two guys hired another friend to help develop the app—an app where you supposedly wouldn't have to worry about taking responsibility for what you send, because it would disappear (like we wish all our problems would do).

But as with many tech start-ups, conflict occurred, and two of the original three guys began plotting to cut the other guy out of the company. This guy caught wind of it and began documenting conversations. This documentation found its way into the courtroom, revealing a little more than these guys probably intended, comments like:

- "The girls are amazing, dude."
- "So it's like, the best way to sext, basically."
- "Uhhhh, let's be honest. What b**ch ever wants anyone to get hold of her pictures?"

I skipped all the f-bombs from these transcripts. But basically, it was obvious these guys were trying to develop an app where you could send pictures you would never want anyone else seeing. (Take a peek at these documents for yourself. Just Google "emails show betrayal at heart of Snapchat."[2])

The biggest problem with the idea behind Snapchat, aside from the fact that these guys were pervs, is the next fact I want to share with you. . .

2. Snapchat pictures don't always disappear.

Sure, it might seem like your snap disappeared right after your friends looked at your picture, video, and/or text. But those pictures you snapped were far more permanent than you thought.

Snapchat's original claim that the pics "disappear" was far from the truth.

In fact, back in 2014, the Federal Trade Commission (FTC), in its efforts to ensure that companies market their apps truthfully, actually charged Snapchat for deceiving its users. Here's a glimpse at the official press release:

> Snapchat, the developer of a popular mobile messaging app, has agreed to settle Federal Trade Commission charges that it deceived consumers with promises about the disappearing nature of messages sent through the service. According to the FTC's complaint, Snapchat made multiple misrepresentations to consumers about its product that stood in stark contrast to how the app actually worked.[3]

Snapchat has had several issues.

First, your friends can easily take a screenshot of whatever you send them. Chances are you know this because, thanks to the FTC's intervention, Snapchat now tells you whenever someone takes a screenshot of one of your pics. Maybe you have witnessed someone send something revealing or embarrassing only to have the pic captured with a screenshot by a friend. Once it's out there. . .*it's out there.*

Second, even if your friends never take a screenshot of your pics, in many cases those pics still could be accessed by a tech nerd who knows where to look on a mobile device.[4] Some of these tech nerds have even developed "Snapchat recovery tools" to help Snap users recover those pics that supposedly "disappeared." Most of these app developers explain that the pics don't actually disappear but are simply buried deep inside your device. A simple Google search will provide Snap users with numerous options to recover pics that were supposed to have been temporary.[5] Such recovery apps have even been available in the iTunes App Store and on Google Play. The FTC reported, "On Google Play alone, ten of these applications have been downloaded as many as 1.7 million times."[6]

That's a lot of people saving these "disappearing pics."

Third, the pics you send are traveling through Snapchat's server, and the Snap execs have access to them. Take a peek for yourself. Look up Snapchat's "Terms of Service." You'll quickly discover that they can "access, review, and screen" your content anytime they want. You agreed to it. This should cause a girl to think twice before she sends a "disappearing" pic of herself in her underwear to a close friend, thinking, *No one but this one friend will see this photo*. Realize that a guy with full access to a server in Venice, California, can see your pic. Maybe even the same guy who the courts have documented saying, "The girls are amazing, dude!"

Of course Snapchat will tell you that only two guys have access to those pics, and the pics are deleted after they are opened (yet stay on the server for thirty days if any of the recipients don't open them). Snapchat admitted that in a matter of a few months they had "turned over unopened snaps to the authorities on about a dozen occasions in response to search warrants."[7] Sad story after sad story where someone takes a picture of something inappropriate or even illegal, all the while thinking, *these pics will disappear*, only to discover later that said pics are Exhibit A in the case against them.

Bottom line: The pics you snap don't just magically disappear. Consider the advice I offered earlier in the book. Don't take pictures of anything you wouldn't want Grandma, your future boss, or Jesus to see.

SO IS SNAPCHAT BAD?

Is the Internet bad? It's the largest database of porn available. It also provides extremely helpful Bible study tools and platforms where you can communicate with your grandma.

Is your TV bad? Your TV screen can show you all sorts of inappropriate programming. . .or that heartwarming Christmas movie your family watches together every year.

Snapchat has become a communication tool that is used for good and bad, depending on the user. And guess what? I'm not going to tell you what you should do. You are the one who has to make these choices in life. My goal is to give you reliable information so you can make wise decisions.

If you are questioning whether using Snapchat is wise, here are some questions you might want to ask yourself:

- What is my motivation in using Snapchat? Do I simply enjoy the convenience of messaging my friends with pics, text, and creative filters, or am I using it because I don't want the accountability if the wrong person were to see the pics and messages I've sent?

- What would my parents and others think if they found all of my Snapchat correspondence? Am I living a life of integrity?
- Is Snapchat a tool I use for good?
- Am I ever tempted to look at inappropriate Snapchat stories?
- Does Snapchat ever lead me into temptation to make decisions that harm me, my relationship with others, and even my relationship with God?

How do you know if Snapchat is for you?

Consider its inception—a group of guys who wanted less accountability for their actions. *I wish I could send irresponsible photos but never suffer the consequences of being irresponsible.* Sadly, that's just not how life works. The photos you take and the messages you post can come back to haunt you. It happens all the time.

I've met literally hundreds of teenagers who made some very poor decisions after hearing the words, "No one will ever know."

Jesus cast some light on this in His conversation with a Pharisee in the book of John. Jesus said:

> *"God's light came into the world, but people loved the darkness more than the light, for their actions were evil. All who do evil hate the light and refuse to go near it for fear their sins will be exposed. But those who do what is right come to the light so others can see that they are doing what God wants."* (John 3:19–21)

Wow. Let those words sink in for a moment. Jesus basically said, "People don't want to step into the light because they know it will expose their actions." That makes a lot of sense when you think about it. Who wants to be bad out in the open? People prefer to keep bad behaviors under the radar. People prefer any record of those bad behaviors would just. . .*disappear*.

QUESTIONS TO PONDER

1. What do you think of Snapchat?
2. Why do you think Snapchat has grown so popular?
3. According to the passage above, why is it that people love darkness more than light?
4. Why don't people want their sins exposed?
5. What are some of the ways people "refuse to go near the light" today, for fear "their sins will be exposed"?
6. What are the dangers you notice about Snapchat?
7. Do you think using Snapchat would be wise for you? Why or why not?

SOMETHING TO THINK ABOUT

It's sad that such a fun app was so misleading from the beginning. The whole idea of posting pictures with no consequences was not only unwise but also far from the truth.

Here's the funny part. Experts have made the point that *texting* is actually more private than Snapchat messages. Really! Here's why. The Federal Communications Commission calls texting a private exchange between two devices, and someone would need a search warrant to access it. Snapchat, on the other hand, is an exchange on a public server. When someone uses the app, they are agreeing to communicate over an insecure network. So Snapchat users are actually not protected legally from having all their conversations and pics accessed.

If you're looking for a way to avoid consequences, you're out of luck. Here's an idea: Only post pics and messages you wouldn't mind the world seeing!

As for using Snapchat. . .you decide.

Tip #11

Reevaluate your screen time.
Trimming hours

*H*ow many hours per day do you think you are connected to some type of entertainment media or technology?

Think about it for a moment. If you add up all your screen time, social media, video games, music, TV, YouTube—all of it—how many hours would it be?

A bunch of researchers did the math recently in their exhaustive study of thousands of teens (thirteen to eighteen years old) and tweens (eight to twelve years old) and discovered these daily averages:

Teenagers: 8 hours 56 minutes
Tweens: 5 hours 55 minutes

Sound like a lot? It's an interesting figure to add up in your own mind. Try it. Add up how much time you spend each day. . .

_____ Watching TV/DVDs/videos/Netflix
_____ Listening to music
_____ Playing video, computer, or mobile games
_____ Using social media
_____ Browsing websites
_____ Doing other activities on a computer or mobile device

_____ Reading magazines or books (categorized as "entertainment media")

_____ Video-chatting

_____ Going to the movies

Here are the daily averages for teenagers:

Watching TV/DVDs/videos/Netflix:	2 hours 38 minutes
Listening to music:	1 hour 54 minutes
Playing video, computer, or mobile games:	1 hour 21 minutes
Using social media:	1 hour 11 minutes
Browsing websites:	36 minutes
Other activities on computer or mobile device:	32 minutes
Reading magazines or books:	28 minutes
Video-chatting:	13 minutes
Going to the movies:	03 minutes
TOTAL:	**8 hours 56 minutes**[1]

Of course, times varied. Some kids exceed these numbers by a long shot, soaking in huge amounts of video streaming, music, and social media. Think about it. How much time do you spend on Netflix or YouTube alone? What about watching stories on your favorite app? Sometimes those minutes add up to hours.

Other kids might be low in one area but high in another. For example, you might not spend a lot of time watching traditional TV but absorb high doses of music and social media. In the same way, some kids don't spend a lot of time on social media but devote hours each day to gaming.

All in all, the average teen spends about nine hours a day digesting this stuff, about six hours of it screen time (because music, for example, isn't screen time, and it's usually played in the background).

Six hours a day staring at screens!

Have you considered the effects of all this screen time?

One of the consequences is poor health. Researchers recently set out to see how the fitness of American kids compared to the fitness of kids from other countries.[2] When compared with kids from countries all over the world, metropolitan and rural, rich and poor, American kids ranked almost dead last: specifically forty-seventh out of fifty.

If you travel the world like I do, you'll hear people in other countries talk about the "fat Americans."

Why is this?

The biggest reason is lack of exercise. And it's not surprising. Between school, meals, sleep. . .and nine hours a day of entertainment media, when do we have time?

Experts recommend that kids daily get at least sixty minutes of moderate to vigorous exercise that uses the big muscles of the body (and they say twenty minutes of it should make you huff and puff). Do you average at least an hour a day of this kind of activity? If not, how are you going to fit exercise in?

Your family doctor would tell you to trim screen time. In fact, your pediatrician would tell *anyone* averaging six hours a day of screen time to make some big changes.

Don't take my word for it. The journal *Pediatrics* has instructed your pediatrician to tell your mom and dad the following: "Limit the amount of total entertainment screen time to less than 1 to 2 hours per day."[3]

Don't get mad at me. I didn't say it. But yeah, moving from six hours to just one or two hours is a huge decrease for most young people.

Is this even possible?

What would trimming screen time look like in your average day?

QUESTIONS TO PONDER

1. Did the fact that kids spend an average of six to nine hours a day using entertainment media surprise you? Why or why not?

2. Do you think those numbers accurately depict you and your friends? Explain.

3. Are there any areas where you spend *more* than the average time? If so, which ones?

4. Are there any areas where you spend less time?

5. How do you measure up with the recommended hour of exercise each day? How's that working for you?

6. Why do you think doctors are recommending only one to two hours a day of screen time? What would that look like in your life?

7. What is something you can do, starting this week, to make sure you aren't digesting too much screen time?

SOMETHING TO THINK ABOUT

How is it even possible to decrease screen time in a world where everyone carries a screen in their pocket?

What are we supposed to do—move into a little cabin in the mountains?

Try discovering some tech-free activities you enjoy. I find that teenagers are often surprised how fun it is to be "social" without social media. My daughters would often go to their grandparents' house (just down the street from us) and invite their friends over to hang out at the pool all day. They would swim and lie out in the sun during the day; then I'd light a big fire in an outdoor fire pit at night and we'd roast marshmallows. Funny, the phones didn't even come out much because there was so much "social" right there in the backyard.

Where are places you can experience that? (We'll highlight some more in the next chapter.)

The world is beginning to experience "constant connectivity overload." As much as we all love our devices, we're realizing we need an occasional rest from the bombardment of information.

Let's consider what this kind of rest actually looks like in the next chapter.

Tip #12

Frequent tech-free zones.
Looking for space

When my kids were in high school, they decided to go on a mission trip with their entire youth group during Easter break. Over seventy kids made plans to go down to the inner city of Los Angeles to feed the homeless and serve the poor.

The youth pastor in charge of the trip always required some intense training to prepare for the week of service. No one knew exactly what the training would involve this particular year, but they had heard stories from students who attended previous training sessions.

The day came when the training requirements would be announced. All the students and parents gathered for a meeting six weeks prior to the trip. The youth pastor didn't waste any time getting to the point.

"This year in preparation for our trip, we're all going to do a media fast. That means no phone, no Internet, no social media, no TV, no music. . .nothing."

The kids all gasped.

"No way!"

I thought there was going to be a riot.

Finally one kid blurted out, "How long?"

The youth pastor smiled. "One month."

The room erupted in sheer chaos. Kids were throwing up their hands in protest.

"This is ridiculous!"

"I'm not going!"

The youth pastor tried to calm everyone down. When the room finally quieted to a dull murmur, the youth pastor explained, "I'm not saying media is bad. I've just decided we need a rest from it. This way we can concentrate on what's important as we prepare our minds and our hearts to serve God on this mission trip."

Then he dropped another bomb.

"Moms and dads, it would be unfair for you to be watching TV in the other room while your kids fast, so we want you to do it, too."

The room erupted again. This time, the parents were freaking out.

When all was said and done, a few students dropped out, but most families agreed to give it a try. Our family was one of those who begrudgingly gave it a shot.

I remember the first morning of the media fast. Everyone loaded into the car, and I routinely turned on the radio. My kids immediately protested. "Dad! The fast!"

I quickly turned it off. "My bad."

It was like living in a different country. We didn't know what to do with ourselves. We were used to simmering in entertainment media all throughout the day. Living without it was like living without. . . *air*!

A couple of days passed. The initial shock was wearing off, but we were still adjusting to the change, like a poodle wearing an uncomfortable new Christmas sweater.

After dinner each night our kids would finish their homework and wander downstairs, bored out of their minds. "So what should we do?"

We would shrug our shoulders. "I don't know—what

do you wanna do?"

Night after night we found ourselves going outside, throwing the ball for the dog, playing catch, gathering around the fireplace, and playing games.

I won't try to mislead you. It was hard! But after about a week we actually were having some fun.

"Dad! Take us to Dairy Queen!"

"Why?"

"Because there's nothing else to do!"

Next thing you know our family was sitting around the table at Dairy Queen laughing and talking for *waaaaay* longer than usual. . .because we literally had nothing else to do.

At first we hated it. But honestly, it grew on us.

It changed us.

One month eventually passed.

The day the fast was over, I think we watched the entire *Lord of the Rings* trilogy. Yeah. . .all day! A massive media binge. The kids weren't paying attention during the entire first film; they were returning two thousand texts.

But then something interesting happened the next few days.

We struggled returning to normal.

My kids actually wanted to continue some of what we started. Not all of it—they enjoy their devices. But they wanted the board games, the puzzles, the trips to Dairy Queen. . .the *conversations.*

So that's when we started "No-Tech Tuesday" in our house. It wasn't anything crazy; we just declared that after school on Tuesday once homework was finished, we'd use no media for the night. No TV, no phones, no music, *nothing.* We usually sat around the fireplace and read or played board games. (I became quite good at Uno.)

And we all really enjoyed our time together.

I'm not going to lie and tell you that we don't use our phones anymore.

I'm not going to tell you we sold our TV or stopped listening to music. We didn't.

I'm not going to try to convince you that entertainment media is all bad.

What I am going to suggest is that sometimes we need to take a rest from all of it and focus on what's important. And nothing is more important than your relationship with God and your relationship with others.

When our family went on the media fast, it literally changed us. It forced us to recognize what was truly important. We liked TV. We liked music. We liked our phones. But we realized even though we thoroughly *enjoy* all those things, we didn't really *need* any of those things. In all honesty, all we needed was God and each other.

TECH-FREE ZONES

The world is slowly beginning to recognize that our phones can interfere with relationships. Magazines, newspapers, and business journals are featuring articles about managing the world of constant connectivity and recommending "tech-free zones."

Most experts aren't recommending people destroy their phones or pack their bags and move to Amish Pennsylvania; they're just recommending some rest from the continuous pings and interruptions.

Last year the *Today Show* aired a feature segment on smartphone obsession. They asked a group of teenagers to try an experiment for one week. Students at Black Hills High School in Washington State gave it a try: no smartphones, no social media, no Internet, only laptops for homework. They each turned in their smartphone and were given a flip phone for emergencies.

A few days into the fast, the students shared their experiences.

- "So far I have done all my chores."
- "I started reading a book last night."
- "I'm getting a lot more homework done."
- "I actually learned a song on my guitar."
- "It's made me hang out with family more often, so it's been nice."[1]

The decision to be tech-free had its benefits.

"Tech-free" comes in many forms. Maybe one of these is worth trying:

- *A complete media fast.* Maybe for a day. . .maybe for a week. You decide.
- *No-Tech Tuesdays.* No phone, Internet, or entertainment media on Tuesdays after school.
- *No tech at the table.* The discipline to keep meals free of interruptions.
- *Tech-free outdoor adventures.* Hiking, cycling, boating, skiing. . .fun activities without the interruption of technology.
- *Hot tubbing.* Who needs tech when you're surrounded by friends and family in hot bubbling H_2O!

Give some of these ideas a try. What's the worst that can happen? You might actually become closer to someone.

And if your parents or family don't want to do it, why not try it with a group of friends? Maybe they'll appreciate the connection they feel when you all practice something as simple as "no tech at the table" during lunch.

In the Bible, Luke tells a story of two sisters who wanted to connect with Jesus, so they invited Him over for dinner. Jesus came to their house, sat down, and began talking with them. One of the sisters sat and talked, but the other became so involved in the meal preparation that she missed out on connecting with Jesus.

Here's the funny part. She actually came to Jesus and complained that she was doing all the work. Take a peek at the story:

> *But Martha was distracted by all the preparations that had to be made. She came to him and asked, "Lord, don't you care that my sister has left me to do the work by myself? Tell her to help me!"*
>
> *"Martha, Martha," the Lord answered, "you are worried and upset about many things, but few things are needed—or indeed only one. Mary has chosen what is better, and it will not be taken away from her."* (Luke 10:40–42 NIV)

When I read this story recently, I noticed two things.

First, Martha was distracted. Is cooking dinner a bad thing? Not at all. But Martha let it become a distraction from connecting with Jesus. Isn't it funny how we can let almost anything become a distraction?

Second, her distraction caused her to begin worrying. I love Jesus' words to Martha. "You are worried and upset about many things." I think Jesus could say the same thing to me at different times in my life. Martha was letting the distractions of life cause her worry and anxiety. So Jesus was honest with her. It's almost like He said to her, "Martha, you're so distracted with dinner preparations that you're missing the dinner! Forget dinner! Order a pizza, sit down next to your sister, and start enjoying the whole reason you began cooking dinner in the first place—so we could hang out together!"

Are you distracted from what's important?

QUESTIONS TO PONDER

1. Have you ever gone without your phone or technology for a lengthy time? What happened?
2. How would you respond if your teacher or youth pastor challenged you to give up your phone, Internet, and entertainment media for a few days?
3. Which app, feature, or form of entertainment would you miss the most?
4. Is there a time of day you could try putting your phone away? When?
5. What will you do if your family and friends aren't excited about trying tech-free moments?
6. In the Bible story, what was Martha distracted by? Is it wrong to cook dinner?
7. What was Jesus' advice to her in verse 42? What is the "one thing" worth being concerned about?
8. How does this story relate to the ways we become distracted today?
9. What distractions might be keeping you from focusing on what's important?

SOMETHING TO THINK ABOUT

When my oldest two kids went off to college, my daughter Ashley, seventeen years old at the time, was the only kid in the house. One Tuesday night we were hanging out in the family room reading by the fire, and my other daughter Alyssa called from her dorm room. I answered the phone.

"Hey, baby. Whatcha doing?"

"Homework," she replied. "What are you guys doing?"

"Oh, you know," I said. "No-Tech Tuesday. We're just sitting around the fire. Mom and I are reading, and Ashley's doing homework."

Alyssa sighed. "Oh man. I miss No-Tech Tuesday. I wish we would have done that more!"

Who'dathunkit!

Tip #13

Friend Mom or Dad.
Connecting with the people who matter

Which is better:

Caring parent: A parent who is interested in where you are on Friday night, who your friends are, and what you're doing on your phone.

Neglectful parent: A mom or dad who doesn't care where you go or who you hang out with. They'd rather not be bothered.

I've worked with kids for over twenty-five years and met examples from each group of parents. Sadly, far more from the second group.

It's interesting. Those kids who have caring parents act a little bit fickle. They welcome the love and security, but when they grow into adolescence and become more independent, they often try to wiggle free from any boundaries, even if the boundaries are helpful. Their mind-set seems to be, *I'll gladly accept your care, but not your meddling*.

In frustration, these kids with caring parents will often exclaim, "I wish you'd just leave me alone!"

They don't even realize what they're saying.

Ask a kid who has a neglectful parent. They'll tell you. Kids who come from homes where Mom or Dad is absent wish they had a parent who cared enough to actually implement boundaries. They wish they had a mom and dad who'd show up. Kids with neglectful parents recognize their parents' lack of interest and care as a lack of love.

Let's be real. It's nice to be loved and cared for. Getting along with Mom and Dad just becomes a little more difficult when said "care" is expressed primarily in rules and regulations, and very little effort is put into the relationship.

Guess what—you can have a huge impact on your relationship with your parents. You have much more influence than you think. Yes, it's a two-way street, and I can't promise you that your parents will always respond perfectly. (In fact, if your parents are like me, I can promise they *won't* always respond perfectly.) But chances are, if you put effort into your relationship with your parents, they will reciprocate with positive efforts of their own.

Let me put it another way. The more energy you put into your relationship with your parents, the greater your reward. Relationships truly are rewarding. And when you get to the point where you can laugh, talk, and even cry with your parents as you walk through life together, you'll be grateful for your investment!

Believe it or not, most kids want their parents in their lives. Author and social researcher Shaunti Feldhahn surveyed about three thousand teens, asking them about their parents' involvement in their lives. Almost all of them (94 percent) said that "if they could wave a magic wand, the perfect situation would be one in which their parents actively worked to be involved with them."[1]

So here's my simple advice to you in an age when social media is a huge part of relational connections: friend Mom or

Dad. If you live with Grandma, friend Grandma. Friend the people who care for you.

I know, I know. I can hear it now.

"I don't want them spying on my every move."

I hear ya. Don't worry. I'm not suggesting you implant a chip in your neck and give your parents a remote control. In fact, whenever I speak to parents at my parent workshops, I actually don't advise "spy software" (the software parents can put on your phone so they can track your every move). Instead, I encourage parents to put down their own devices and take notice of your interests. That means if you play soccer, they should show up and cheer for you at your games (and maybe even take you to get ice cream afterward). And if you like to play video games, they should sit down with you and play two-player mode.

In the same way, if you're on social media, I would advise your parents to "friend" you and correspond with you in a casual and respectful way.

STALKER MOM

I realize some parents go a little too far with their presence on social media. I remember when my daughter Ashley was ranting about it at dinner one night.

"What is up with these moms? Do they live on their computers?"

We laughed. Ashley frequently had us laughing at the dinner table.

"I'm serious." She named one of her friend's moms. "That woman is on social media every second of the day. She's like 'Big Brother.' She's watching!"

My wife, Lori, gave me "the look"—the look that said I

was supposed to intervene and say something. Something like, "Ashley, stop being disrespectful." But I was laughing too hard.

"Ashley," I finally mustered, "give Stalker Mom a break."

She laughed. "Watch this," she said, ignoring my suggestion. She pulled out her phone. "I'm going to post something right now. Just watch."

Curiosity overwhelmed us. We all got up and gathered around her phone.

Ashley hit "Post," and we watched in suspense.

Two likes appeared. Neither of them Stalker Mom.

Literally about ten seconds passed.

Then. . .a *thumbs-up* emoji.

It was Stalker Mom.

We all howled in laughter. (We're really bad people.)

My daughter isn't alone in her feelings. Young people everywhere don't want Mom and Dad abusing their authority on social media. Researchers out of the University of Michigan studied hundreds of parent-child pairs and asked them questions about the rules they thought families should follow related to social media and technology. The list was very much like you'd expect. "Don't text and drive. Don't have your head buried in your phone when someone is talking with you." But researchers saw another "rule" come up again and again.

"Don't post anything about me on social media without asking me."[2]

It's frustrating when parents post embarrassing pics or rants. It violates trust.

But don't let this be an excuse to sever any "online" relationship with your parents. Relationships undergo conflicts, and a big part of growing up is learning to deal with these conflicts. Don't let rough waters keep you from ever learning to swim.

FIRST TO "FRIEND"

A good way to avoid having a "stalker mom" is to be open and honest with your parents. In fact, initiate conversations and encourage points of connection. When you get Instagram, ask your mom, "Mom, are you on Insta? Follow me." Be the first to friend them. The more you involve your parents in your life, the more they'll trust that you have nothing to hide. (We'll talk about actually having nothing to hide later in this book—Tip #19, "No secrets.")

I'll share something with you that most young people don't know: Most parents aren't stalkers. In fact, most are quite the opposite.

Most parents don't monitor their kids' screen time, social media profiles, texting, etc. Most moms and dads let their kids figure it out for themselves. In fact, a few summers ago the tech company McAfee actually did a study discovering that 74 percent of parents surveyed claimed they can't possibly keep up with all their kids' entertainment media and technology, so they simply "hope for the best."[3]

I tell you this for the same reason I wrote you this book. *You are the one* who is ultimately responsible for your behaviors on social media and your mobile devices. In most situations, Mom or Dad *won't* be looking over your shoulder.

It's probably up to you to initiate any accountability with Mom and Dad.

It's most likely your decision to include—or not include—your parents in your world of social media. You have to make that call.

Take the step toward open communication.

Friend Mom, Dad, Grandma, Auntie. . .those who love and care for you.

THINGS WILL GO WELL

What if I promised you that things will go well for you? That's a pretty cool promise.

Most people don't notice, but one of the Ten Commandments includes this promise along with it. Paul points this out later in the Bible in the book of Ephesians. In fact, my guess is you've heard this verse quoted numerous times. The question is, did you notice the promise?

> *Children, obey your parents because you belong to the Lord, for this is the right thing to do. "Honor your father and mother." This is the first commandment with a promise: If you honor your father and mother, "things will go well for you, and you will have a long life on the earth."* (Ephesians 6:1–3)

Paul doesn't just tell young people to obey their parents because "I told you so!" He actually gives a convincing reason. "Things will go well for you."

Think about it. Have you ever had a friend who was constantly disrespecting their parents, rebelling against them, and fighting them at every turn? I promise you, things are not "going well for them." It's not fun to be in the midst of that situation on either side. Not only is honoring your mom and dad the right thing to do, but it creates peaceful living.

Sadly, Mom and Dad aren't always perfect; sometimes they really mess up. But this doesn't mean you can't show them respect.

Whenever I talk about the subject of honoring parents, some kid will always ask me, "What if my mom or dad told me to do something morally wrong or to break the law?"

Sometimes that happens. And if it did, you could respectfully tell them why you won't do what they told you to do. *Respectfully.*

But for most kids, that doesn't happen. Instead, what sometimes happens is that kids get their phone taken away because they broke the rules. . .and then they act like their parents violated their constitutional rights. (You know it's true!)

"Honor your father and mother"—even if they are being difficult or unfair. Your honor and respect will help you build bonds with them that will last a lifetime.

QUESTIONS TO PONDER

1. Why do you think some moms and dads "stalk" their kids on social media? Is this right?
2. Why are so many young people resistant to having their parents connect with them on social media? Is this fair?
3. How can a parent show care and effectively teach you responsibility on social media?
4. According to the passage from Ephesians, what happens if you honor your father and mother? Why do you think God said this?
5. What are some ways things could "go well for you" if you honored your parents?
6. What is a way you can honor your mom and dad in the world of social media?
7. What is something you can do this week to show them honor?

SOMETHING TO THINK ABOUT

I'm forty-six years old as I write this, and my dad is seventy-five. My parents live half a mile down the road from our house, and we visit them several times a week. We pray with them once a week, and I go out to dinner with my Dad on Wednesday nights. We're. . .friends.

When I was sixteen, I probably never would have foreseen that my dad and I would be such good friends. But my parents have been there for me more times than I can count.

Family sticks together.

I can tell you honestly—I don't hang out with even one of the friends I hung out with in high school. I still know a couple and keep in touch, but I don't regularly hang out with any of them.

But I talk with my dad almost every day.

Chances are your parents and family will be around far longer than your friends. Chances are they'll bail you out financially once or twice when you need a loan. . .or if you do something stupid.

Your parents might even turn out to be some of your best friends.

Might be a good idea to "friend" them if that's the case.

Tip #14

Dissect your entertainment media.
Rethinking the music, TV, and videos you watch

On April 15, 1983, a film hit the screens that actually changed your mom's wardrobe. The movie was *Flashdance*. It didn't matter if women saw the film or not. If you were female and alive in the early '80s, you bought a pair of leg warmers and cut a big hole out of the top of your biggest sweatshirt and wore it off the shoulder. Every girl wanted the *Flashdance* look.

Guys would never do something like this, right?

Think again.

Literally one year later a TV show launched called *Miami Vice*, introducing two Miami cops with stylish pastel suits and sleek exotic cars no one on a police salary could ever afford. Not only did the show change television. . .it changed your dad's wardrobe. It didn't matter if you were from Texas or Jersey. Everyone loved the suave looks of Detectives Sonny Crockett and Ricardo Tubbs. In fact, by 1985, almost every teen guy was dressed exactly like Crockett or Tubbs at their school dance (look at your dad's photo album from the late '80s—you'll see).

This was way back in the '80s, before everyone carried a screen in their pocket. But the screen's influence was undeniable.

While you have that photo album out, turn to the '90s and look at your mom's or your aunt's haircut. I bet one of them had "the Rachel." Yes, Jennifer Aniston's character in *Friends* was such a beloved icon that practically every young woman began asking their hairstylist, "Can you give me that haircut

Rachel has on *Friends*?" People couldn't get enough of their weekly dose of *Friends* (no Netflix binges back then).

Fast-forward to today. How is it that every five-year-old in America can sing the words to "Let It Go" word for word? How come every teenager can imitate a South Korean pop star named Psy dancing like he's riding an invisible horse—"Gangnam Style"—and that was way back in 2012 (when only 50 percent of Americans had a smartphone)? Maybe for the same reason they can sing "Chocolate Rain."

The power of entertainment media is undeniable. It's loaded with fashion icons and packed with imitable behaviors.

Don't worry. This isn't where I begin a lecture about how all TV and music is bad. To the contrary, I really enjoy entertainment media. In fact, my youngest daughter, Ashley, and I often end up having lengthy conversations about our favorite movies or nostalgic songs. Her taste in music is broad, so she makes amazing playlists. I even pay for her Spotify account just so we can share our lists.

But as much as I love music and screen entertainment, I'd be a fool not to notice its sway over people's thoughts and behaviors. The arts have always been a powerful medium for tickling people's emotions and nudging them to act out. Today's entertainment media influences your mind more than you might guess.

Music, for example, is known to soothe or excite people. But recent studies also reveal that music can help people remember, even boosting memory in Alzheimer's patients.[1] If words are put to music, people are far more likely to remember what they heard. . .and how it made them feel. In the same way, nostalgic songs can quickly trigger specific memories. Maybe you've experienced this phenomenon when you heard a certain song and immediately thought, *Sixth grade, at the skating rink with. . .*

You probably don't need a scientist to convince you of music's influence. Think about the playlists you have created. Most people create various playlists for diverse moods. You might have an exercise playlist, a peppy or upbeat playlist, and a sad, thoughtful, or melancholy playlist.

Why? Music tends to sway our mood. We admittedly use it that way.

Sadly, music and media can influence our behavior in more ways than just prompting us to wear a torn sweatshirt or a pastel suit. Let's take a quick glimpse at two eye-opening studies.

1. MUSIC'S INFLUENCE ON RISKY SEXUAL BEHAVIORS

In 2015 some researchers from the University of Central Florida tackled a project that didn't win them any favors with the music industry.[2] They sought to examine the relationship between sexual content in music lyrics and music videos and the sexual behaviors of young people. In other words, "Do the lyrics of my music or the sexy images in the videos I watch actually make me more likely to have sex or engage in risky sexual activities?"

Earlier studies from the American Academy of Pediatrics had found that "teens who said they listened to lots of music with degrading sexual messages were almost twice as likely to start having intercourse or other sexual activities within the following two years as were teens who listened to little or no sexually degrading music."[3]

So these Florida researchers decided to embark on a similar study with college kids. The results weren't surprising: "Exposure to music containing sexual content is associated with engagement in risky sexual behaviors."[4]

Researchers particularly noticed a link between sexual content in music and "the participants' age at their first sexual encounter, number of sexual partners in the past 12 months, rate of changing sexual partners, and condom use."[5] Bottom line: The more sexually charged the music, the riskier the sexual behaviors.

The study also revealed that music had a greater impact on certain races and ethnicities. Some races were much more likely to act out the behaviors they heard through their headphones simply "because they are more likely to view music as an accurate representation of their culture."[6]

The majority of young people showed a very broad taste in music, listening to a variety of genres. Sexual content was found in most of these genres. In my own research, I examine the top ten of the Billboard Hot 100 songs all throughout the year. Last month when I analyzed them, I found seven of the ten songs were about romantic relationships, six of the songs mentioned specific sexual situations, and three of them actually referred to male or female genitalia.

If this is the top music, and sexually laced lyrics have proven to encourage risky sexual behaviors, it's no surprise the Centers for Disease Control recently posted a press release revealing that sexually transmitted diseases (STDs) are at an unprecedented high in the United States.[7]

But raunchy music isn't just affecting us physically; it's affecting us emotionally. Let's look at a second study.

2. SEXUALIZATION

Many of you have already seen studies showing that the simple act of reading a fashion magazine or looking at images of models has a negative effect on women's and girls' self-esteem.[8] Girls think, *How come I don't look like that?*

Sadly, these images also convince girls of something else— you need to be sexy!

In a world where sexy images seep through every Wi-Fi signal and dance across our screens, the natural tendency is to value ourselves by our sex appeal.

She's wearing really revealing clothes and is acting sensual. . . and she's got millions of views on YouTube! Maybe that's how I should act.

Some doctors have actually labeled this phenomenon, calling it "sexualization." The American Psychological Association released a report titled "The Sexualization of Girls," defining sexualization as "when a person's value comes only from her/his sexual appeal or behavior, to the exclusion of other characteristics, and when a person is sexually objectified, e.g., made into a thing for another's sexual use."[9]

The effects of sexualization might have hit you at a young age, especially considering how almost every child actor/singer you may have enjoyed has fallen prey to this line of thinking. Not just Miley swinging buck naked on a wrecking ball, or Demi singing about kissing a girl for the first time, concluding, "If it's wrong, if it's right, I don't care." Each year of your childhood could have provided plenty of examples. Consider Selena Gomez's song "Good for You" from a couple of years ago. She sensually sang that she just wanted to look good for a guy, even describing the dress she'd wear "skin-tight". . .before she'd take it off for said guy, leaving it "a mess on the floor."

The song suggests the singer's value is based on her ability to be sexy for a guy and apparently to get naked for the guy.

No sexy. . .*no guy.*

You don't have to look far to find evidence of this popular line of thinking. Our culture values "sexy." Just turn on your TV. It's dominated by the sexy and the beautiful.

Why?

People like sexy. If marketers show us sexy, we want it.

Lady Gaga readily admits to using these kinds of tactics: "I was nineteen and I was playing a show where I was supposed to debut all this new material," Gaga said. "When I sat down to play I couldn't get everyone to stop talking, so I took off all my clothes. Works every time."[10]

Think about the last music video you saw. How many of the girls featured in the video got that role because of their keen mind or great personality? Even though our world might value these characteristics, the entertainment media we soak in at the rate of nine hours a day doesn't place a high value on inner beauty. Entertainment media values sex appeal.

Girls face this struggle every day—especially on Halloween. As the dad of two girls, I know. It doesn't matter if you want to be a soccer player, a princess, or a pirate. All of those costumes will somehow feature an ultra-short skirt and a plunging neckline. Cady said it well in the movie *Mean Girls*: "In the real world, Halloween is when kids dress up in costumes and beg for candy. In Girl World, Halloween is the one day a year when a girl can dress up like a total slut and no other girls can say anything else about it."[11]

Does sexualization have any negative effects?

According to the research by the American Psychological Association, sexualization has "negative effects in a variety of domains, including cognitive functioning, physical and mental health, sexuality, and attitudes and beliefs."[12]

When girls feel the pressure to feel sexy, the consequences are severe.

We've looked at just two studies about how entertainment media can affect us negatively. Obviously entertainment media provides a wide variety of options, some good and some not so good. Some shows or lyrics might not have any sexual content whatsoever but instead may be filled with profanity or violence. That's why it's important to stay connected to venues where you can glean truth and learn lasting values. Then you'll recognize injustice when you see it and be able to identify lies when you hear them. After all, someday you'll be making all these entertainment media decisions on your own.

What will you choose to watch then?

ENTERTAINMENT MEDIA DIET

Our phone never came with a warning label:

CAUTION: Mindlessly soaking in popular entertainment media has been known to convince people they aren't sexy enough or sexual enough. Please absorb this entertainment media at your own risk.

So how can we guard ourselves from being brainwashed by our own entertainment? That's a good question. But maybe the question you should be asking is, "What do I really believe?"

If you *don't* believe in God or the Bible, then simply consider the research you've read above. It's not from the Bible or any religious journals; instead, it represents the findings of many doctors and researchers who recognize clear consequences when young people don't monitor their own entertainment media diet. So if this is you, then you might want to consider filtering out entertainment media with these deceiving messages.

If you do claim to be a Christian, then you might want to ask yourself what you believe. Because when you truly put your trust in Christ, that key decision will give you a sense of purpose and identity in Him that will help guide all your day-to-day decisions, including your entertainment media diet. No, this ability to make wise choices doesn't kick in instantaneously. God knows you are a work in progress. But when you put your trust in Him, He will actually begin to change the way you think (Romans 12:2). You'll begin to recognize when you encounter music encouraging you to just *let go* or *lose control* or convincing you that you *can't stop* or you *don't gotta think about nothing* (all common phrases from top songs in the last year).

When you encounter this kind of entertainment, you won't freak out or plug your ears screaming. . .but you'll begin to realize the emptiness of it all and steer away from it the next time you hear it. If you have questions, you'll talk with other believers about them, seeking settings where you can soak in truth, not be bombarded with lies.

Your new identity in Christ not only will transform your actions but will point others to Him. When your friends see how you behave, they'll wonder. They might even ask you to give a reason for the "hope" you're demonstrating (1 Peter 3:15–16) in a world that sometimes seems so hopeless.

Paul talks about this "new life with Christ" in Colossians 3, explaining how to get rid of your old ways of thinking and put on a new way of thinking. I encourage you to read it. He finishes that section in verse 17 with this summary: "And whatever you do or say, do it as a representative of the Lord Jesus, giving thanks through him to God the Father."

Pause for a moment and consider the songs you listen to,

the shows you watch, the apps you use, and the online locations you frequent. Do these represent the Lord Jesus?

QUESTIONS TO PONDER
1. What are some fads, trends, or even funny viral videos you remember that had a huge following?
2. What are some songs, TV shows, and videos you really enjoy?
3. Why do you think listening to sexual content in music or watching sensual music videos increases risky sexual behaviors?
4. What are some examples of "sexualization" you notice in the world?
5. Read Colossians 3:1–17. What are some examples of how this passage specifically applies to your own entertainment media diet?
6. What are some specific adjustments you might need to make in your entertainment media diet?
7. How can you live life as a representative of the Lord this week?

SOMETHING TO THINK ABOUT
In this chapter I shared a few common themes found at the top of the music charts. I purposely postponed telling you about something else I observed in those charts because I wanted to conclude with it.

It's interesting. I've been studying music for almost two decades. As a guy who researches and teaches youth culture, I can't possibly ignore what young people are learning from a source they plug into an average of about two hours a day. And the more I study popular music, the more I see two overwhelming themes flowing from the lyrics:

1. Live for the moment!
2. Why am I feeling so much pain?

Think about those themes for a moment. The most popular songs at any given moment fall into one of two categories: (1) *Do what feels right. . .right now*, and (2) *Why does this hurt so bad?*

When I cited themes earlier in this chapter, I shared that seven of the ten songs were about romantic relationships, six mentioned specific sexual situations, and three actually referred to male or female genitalia. When I examined those songs even closer, I found that nine of the ten fell into the two categories I mentioned: living for the moment or feeling pain. Specifically, four of the songs were about doing what feels good in the moment (mostly about giving in to sexual temptation), and five were about suffering because of a broken relationship.

Let that sink in for a moment.

Do you see a connection?

One type of song preaches, "Live for the moment, give in to temptation, lose control, don't think about anything, just give in to your desires and hope there are no consequences." The other type of song cries out, "Why does this hurt so bad?"

Hmm. Read that paragraph again.

What's in your phone?

SOMETHING TO TRY THIS WEEK
1. Read Colossians 3:1–17 every day this week, asking God to speak to you specifically about your entertainment media.
2. Pray and ask God two questions: "Is there something

I need to remove from my entertainment menu?" and "How can I better represent You in everything I say and do?"

3. Look for places where you can soak in truth and not be bombarded with lies: church, church youth group, Bible studies, and friendships with others who hold the same biblical values.

Tip #15

Pause.
Remembering to think before you post

*J*ustin never realized his words would come back to haunt him until US marshals showed up at his work and arrested him.

It began when Justin thoughtlessly posted something on social media:

I think I'ma SHOOT UP A KINDERGARTEN

He quickly followed the post with:

AND WATCH THE BLOOD OF THE INNOCENT RAIN DOWN.

Justin didn't give it another thought when he went to bed that night. But the post stirred up some attention.

Someone stumbled onto the post, took a screenshot, and contacted the authorities. It didn't take long for them to locate Justin, who happened to live within one hundred yards of an elementary school.

Law enforcement personnel had been criticized countless times for ignoring similar warnings that turned out to be catastrophic, so they didn't take any chances this time. A judge issued a warrant, and Justin was arrested.

Here's where many people thought Justin would receive a warning, a mere "hand slap," and maybe spend one night in jail. That's what happens in the movies, right? Dad bails out the kid the next morning, warns him, "Don't do that again," and then everything's fine.

But this wasn't the movies.

Justin claimed he was just joking with his friends. It's the defense almost every teen uses in these situations. "It was a joke!"

Unfortunately, no one was laughing now.

Justin's words carried far more weight than he ever intended. He was charged with a third-degree terroristic threat, which carries a penalty of two to ten years.

Justin spent months in jail while lawyers tried to convince the prosecutors he was a good kid and his words were harmless. It was during this time that the unthinkable happened. While the lawyers battled, Justin was sexually assaulted in jail. Sadly, not a rare occurrence.

Shortly after, Justin was put on suicide watch.

"He's very depressed," his dad told CNN. "He's very scared and he's very concerned that he's not going to get out. He's pretty much lost all hope."[1]

Justin finally was released after an anonymous donor posted his bail for half a million dollars, temporarily freeing him from jail until trial. As of the writing of this book, he is still awaiting a pretrial hearing.[2]

I don't tell this story to try to scare you about random unforeseen circumstances. Our actions have consequences. And if you threaten to kill people, *even if you're joking*, chances are you'll see a jail cell. Our words carry incredible weight.

Last year a fourteen-year-old boy in Houston thought it would be funny to post a clown-related threat to a school nearby. So he posted something on social media saying he would shoot up a local school with his "clown friend." The boy was arrested for making a terrorist threat.[3]

A seventeen-year-old boy in New York City was arrested on similar charges for a Facebook post where he threatened that if someone ran up on him, "he gonna get blown down." The post was followed by the emojis of a policeman and three guns. Authorities saw this as a credible threat and arrested him.[4]

A fourteen-year-old girl was arrested for tweeting the following:

@AmericanAir hello my name's Ibrahim and I'm from Afghanistan. I'm part of Al Qaida and on June 1st I'm gonna do something really big bye.

Just minutes later she pleaded with the airline, "I'm just a girl," claiming it was a joke made by her friend. It didn't matter. The words were out there.[5]

My point is simple: Think before you post.

I've already touched on this in earlier chapters. We've talked about how pics stick and how Snapchat images aren't as temporary as many think. In those chapters I encouraged you to avoid posting images and content you wouldn't want the world to see, and now I'm reinforcing that point with a little guidance on how to avoid regretful posts.

The answer is in one simple word: *Pause.*

It's not an oversimplification. You'd be surprised how many mistakes you can avoid when you merely stop and take a moment to think before you act.

HINDSIGHT

Have you ever regretted something you posted? One survey found that 57 percent of Americans who use social media have posted something they regretted afterward. Some do this quite often. Moreover, 20 percent of young people say they post or text something they regret about once a week.[6]

That's a lot of regret!

If you're like most people, after you make a mistake, you rethink the situation and consider other ways you should have handled it. Often this time of pondering helps us see the situation more clearly. It's like the old saying, "Hindsight is 20/20." The best course of action seems much more obvious when you have time to mull it over.

Here's the funny part.

It's not always the *hindsight* that provides the wisdom. It's often the time we spend mulling it over. In other words, if we would just take a little time to think things through in the first place, maybe we wouldn't do stupid stuff!

Most regretful posts happen "in the moment." Someone says something that makes us upset, and we post emotionally instead of thoughtfully.

So my advice to you is simple: Pause.

If you find yourself regretting your posts frequently (maybe even weekly), then just pause. Force yourself to literally put down your device and wait awhile before posting a response. In fact, sleep on it. Chances are, when you wake up, you won't be as emotional and "in the moment." And you might save yourself a lot of grief.

I bet all the individuals whose stories I shared earlier in this chapter wish they would have paused.

The Bible offers some particularly relevant advice that we

can apply to posting on social media. It's found in the book of James: "Everyone should be quick to listen, slow to speak and slow to become angry" (James 1:19 NIV).

Today that verse could be worded, "Be quick to think and slow to type with your thumbs."

Perhaps if we weren't so quick to post, we'd save ourselves a lot of regret.

QUESTIONS TO PONDER

1. Have you ever regretted something you posted? What happened?
2. What would you do differently if you could do that situation over?
3. Have you ever unintentionally hurt someone with something you posted? What happened?
4. Do you think any of the young people in this chapter foresaw the probable consequences of their words? Should they have? Explain.
5. What did James mean by "slow to speak" in James 1:19?
6. What might that look like in relation to social media today?
7. What is one way you can avoid regretful posts in the future?

SOMETHING TO THINK ABOUT

As you may have noticed, many regretful posts began as jokes. Those who created these posts quickly realized two things:

1. Threats are never treated as jokes.
2. Your online identity is never private.

That's what countless teenagers discovered the hard way last Halloween when they thought they'd jump on the "creepy clown" bandwagon. Teens were arrested all over the US for making threats to "abduct kids" or "kill someone."

Police don't ignore these threats.

One of the dozens of examples was a Southern California teen who created an anonymous "clown site" on social media, posting that his school was "gonna get hit" tomorrow, so "say your blessings." Even though his name was nowhere on the page, police easily tracked him down and arrested him.[7]

The arresting officers told the news, "We look at all these threats, especially threats to schools, as being very serious, and we treat them that way. That is why we tracked him down and arrested him."[8]

Bail was set at $50,000.

Another fourteen-year-old teen was arrested for making similar criminal threats. Later, he told detectives he just wanted to scare people in order to get social media followers.[9]

It's hard to check your "likes" from a prison cell.

Think before you post. There are some words you can't take back.

Tip #16

Crush criticism and cruelty.
Discovering the power of kind words

His name is Ghyslain Raza. You might not recognize the name, but you've probably seen the video.

The Internet dubbed him "Star Wars kid." The fourteen-year-old enthusiastically twirled a stick around like Darth Maul. No one knows why the video went viral; perhaps it was his steadfast concentration on the task at hand, or the obvious bliss he experienced as he battled invisible enemies.

Some classmates found the video and thought it would be funny to post it. And that's when the story takes a dark turn.

People were beyond cruel. They were heinous.

Raza, now an adult, reflects back to this dark time in his life: "What I saw was mean. It was violent. People were telling me to commit suicide."[1]

The teasing transcended online comments. Fellow students would stand up on tabletops at school and hurl insults at him. The bullying got so bad that he eventually left school to be tutored privately. But he could never escape the online cruelty.

Later that year in an interview with the *Canadian National Post*, he said, "I want my life back."[2]

Sadly, Raza is not alone. You don't have to search far to find a victim of online cruelty. In fact, just scroll through the comment section of any viral video. You'll see a stream of cruel remarks. Social media is packed with cowards in the comment section who obviously have nothing better to do than criticize others.

As part of Dove's self-esteem campaign, the company released a video about selfies in which young girls talked openly about their insecurities in posting pics.[3] It's hard living in a world where any pics you post are subjected to the scrutiny of heartless critics.

One little girl wearing glasses shared what people had commented about her looks. "I look like a twelve-year-old. I look like a boy."

And in a moment of sincerity, she asked, "Why would people say that? It just really hurts."

Online cruelty has driven many to suicide. A thirteen-year-old Missouri girl met a guy online named Josh. Little did she know, "Josh" was actually the mother of one of the girl's ex-friends—a mother with a grudge. Posing as Josh, the mother flirted with the young girl for several weeks. Then she turned mean and informed the girl she didn't want to be friends anymore and that, in fact, the world would be better off without her.

The young girl hung herself.[4]

A mother!

I wrote it before and I'll write it again: Words are powerful.

Whoever first said, "Sticks and stones may break my bones, but words will never hurt me," was *dead wrong*!

Words can build someone up or destroy them. You know this, and I probably don't need to give you thirteen reasons why.

Which would you rather do: build someone up or destroy them?

THE POWER OF KIND WORDS

You don't have to look far in the world of social media to see someone being callous, critical, or cruel. People sometimes do it in a backstabbing way—like subtweets—referring to someone without mentioning them by name.

Don't get sucked into the drama. This is real life, not an MTV reality show. Words can hurt someone far more than they let on. Rare is the person who can rise above the hate and transcend this kind of insensitive talk.

When I was a young boy and first lost my two front teeth, everyone thought it was cute. We've all been there—the huge, gummy gap. Almost a trademark of youth.

But when my "adult teeth" grew in, it wasn't a pretty picture.

You've heard the term *buck teeth*? If you look up those words in the dictionary, you should see a picture of me in fourth grade. My teeth were *huge*! I'm not exaggerating. I would be standing in line at the grocery store with my mom, and I could hear little kids in line behind me asking their moms out loud, "Mom, what's wrong with his teeth?"

I immediately became the target of bullying—something I had never experienced before my "big" teeth came in. I was called every name in the book: Bugs Bunny, Bucky Beaver, Fang Face, Can Opener (that one was actually pretty creative, in retrospect).

Those names killed me.

I remember standing in front of the mirror in my bedroom desperately trying to close my lips and cover my teeth. It didn't work. They stuck out no matter what I did.

If you haven't experienced ridicule, then you might not be aware how much words can hurt. . .or help.

In fourth grade I was hanging out with a friend of mine, a young girl—a *cute* girl—I knew from church. She heard some kids tease me and asked me earnestly, "Do people tease you about your teeth?"

"All the time," I said.

Then she said some of the sweetest words I've ever heard in my lifetime. "I think they're cute." And she kissed me on the forehead.

I'll never forget that moment as a fourth grader. Probably the best moment of my childhood.

Yes, I got kissed by a cute girl! It's hard to discount that moment. But honestly, those four words are what I remember. *"I think they're cute."*

Those words sailed me past every other insult for the next three years of my life (until I finally got braces).

Do you realize the power of kind words?

In my work with teenagers I've heard countless stories of abuse and ridicule. In all those cases I clearly recognize one factor contributing to a teen's ability to stride through those tough times and survive: kind words from one friend.

Funny, most friends probably don't even realize the power of their kind words. But sometimes those words can literally be lifesaving!

This proverb puts it well: "The words of the reckless pierce like swords, but the tongue of the wise brings healing" (Proverbs 12:18 NIV).

I've felt the piercing of reckless words. They feel like a sword. Many of you know the feeling. At the same time, many of you have felt the soothing comfort of kind words. They truly can "bring healing."

Think of a time when someone said something kind to you and you replied, "You just made my day."

Words can "make someone's day."

Words hold incredible power.

QUESTIONS TO PONDER

1. Have you ever witnessed someone being cruel online? What did you notice?
2. Have you ever been the target of online cruelty? What effect did it have on you?
3. Describe a time when you said something or posted something mean and regretted it later.
4. Why do words "pierce like swords"?
5. According to the proverb, whose tongue brings healing? What makes a person "wise" in this way?
6. What are some ways someone could use kind words on social media?
7. What is a way you can be "wise" on social media this week, bringing healing to those you engage in conversation?

SOMETHING TO THINK ABOUT

For years I've heard school officials and child development experts argue about how to prevent bullying. And the conclusions are sometimes hilarious. I think I'm allowed to laugh, since I truly was bullied for years as a kid.

Some experts have come up with (I'm not making this up) anti-bullying backpacks and anti-bullying spray!

Yeah. Seriously.

It's always interesting to hear people talking about bullying. . .when they've never been bullied. It's like someone who has never been in the ocean trying to teach you to surf.

No thanks.

Let me tell you the cure for bullying. Yes, I've seen it work. As a guy who was bullied for years, who speaks to teenagers across the world, and who researches this stuff weekly, I know the cure.

You!

You are the cure. You alone can prevent it by being a friend.

Let me cite just one study. It's an insightful study out of Cambridge University about the "snowball effect" of depression.[5] Basically researchers observed how depression could grow rapidly or "snowball" when subjects were alone. But one component could stop that rapid trajectory of negativity every time.

A friend.

Not even a bunch of friends. One friend was enough to prevent an anxious, withdrawn child from spiraling into a depressed state.

And you can be that friend.

You can post affirmation when everyone else is posting snippy comments, subtweets, and thoughtless banter.

Better yet, you can say kind words to someone's face, when chances are, they might not have heard any kind words all day.

You can make someone's day.

Your kind words might even save a life!

Tip #17

Recognize the distraction.
Texting, driving. . .and killing

I drive about thirty to forty cars a year.

No, I don't work at a car dealership; and no, I don't personally have that many vehicles. I just fly to about three cities a month to speak, and I always drive a rental car for the weekend.

One of the fun aspects of renting cars each month is trying out different makes and models. The car rental company I use actually lets me choose any car on the lot since I'm such a frequent renter.

I've driven all kinds!

Sometimes I grab sleek convertibles or sports cars. Other times I'll choose cars with powerful engines like a Dodge Challenger or a beefy SUV. But most of the time I'll opt for a car with the most accessories so I can charge my phone, sync it to the stereo system, and hear my phone's navigation through the vehicle's speakers.

Regardless, whenever I first get in the car, the first thing I do is look at the steering wheel.

Sounds silly. It's just a circle with grips!

Nope! Not anymore.

When I was in high school, a steering wheel was nothing more than a wheel with maybe a horn. But the more technologically advanced we get, the more we need thumb controls for all our gadgets: *answer call, hang up, voice command, volume, menu, toggle*. . .all on the steering wheel.

Why do we need all these controls?

Because people are dying for their phones.

I'm not speaking metaphorically. They're actually dying.

Car companies have been adding more and more "hands-free" controls each year because people are literally dying due to distracted driving. These automakers are doing everything they can to help us keep our eyes on the road instead of on our phone.

But some people think technology companies should be doing more. For example, a class action lawsuit in my own state of California is going after Apple, claiming the iPhone has caused 52,000 accidents per year and 312 deaths. Lawyers are specifically after the company for not using a "lockout system" that would prevent drivers from texting when the car is moving. They claim Apple "had the technology to prevent texting and driving, but has failed to implement it."[1]

I hardly think it is Apple's fault when people decide to take their eyes off the road just to check for "likes" on their post or to message their friend Christina! Nevertheless, 1.5 million people are "texting and driving" at any given moment. Truly frightening.

Let me quickly point out that the expression "texting and driving" is proving to be outdated. The activity teens engage in the most while driving is social media. In fact, 68 percent of teenagers use apps while driving.[2] And 74 percent of all drivers confess they would use Facebook while driving.[3]

Would you?

Even if you knew your actions could kill someone?

A DEADLY PEEK

How important is it to check that one message?

Apparently it was very important for a seventeen-year-old Minnesota teen who kept looking at her phone while driving. Her three friends actually asked her to get off her phone, but their requests were ignored. Evidence later supported her friends' testimony that she was texting and posting to social media, so much so that she didn't notice a red light.

Her car ran the red light, T-boning a passing minivan in the intersection. The minivan was driven by fifty-four-year-old Charles Maurer who was driving his ten-year-old daughter. Maurer was airlifted to a hospital where he was quickly pronounced dead. His daughter was on life support for ten days before she died.

The seventeen-year-old driver who couldn't stop looking at her phone survived, and now she's facing two counts each of criminal vehicular homicide and criminal vehicular operation, and texting and driving. That doesn't even include the life sentence of "guilt" she'll carry. She immediately began going to counseling.[4]

This story isn't unique. It happens all the time.

A sixteen-year-old Kansas teen was texting while driving and veered off the shoulder of the road. When she corrected the vehicle back onto the road, she swerved into oncoming traffic, hitting another car head-on and killing the driver, a seventy-two-year-old woman. The teen was charged with involuntary manslaughter in the second degree, third-degree assault, and texting while driving. If convicted of the manslaughter charge, the girl faces up to four years in prison plus another year for the assault charge.[5]

A similar case involved an eighteen-year-old San Antonio

girl who killed a thirty-two-year-old father of two whose wife was pregnant with their third. Police were unsure whether to charge the teen driver with criminal charges, so the victim's family filed suit for one million dollars to "try to make a difference and send a message on this important public safety issue."[6]

In each of these stories, the driver is facing a lifetime of enormous consequences for a split-second decision to look at their phone.

Do you think it was worth it?

States all over the US are passing legislation with harsher punishments for texting with, talking on, or even holding a phone. Most states, regardless of size, have suffered far too many accidents and deaths. Even the small state of Iowa reported over a thousand crashes last year alone involving drivers distracted by the use of an electronic device.[7]

It's almost like people don't recognize what a distraction their phones can be.

AN EXPERIMENT

Which is more distracting: texting and driving. . .or drinking and driving?

Car and Driver magazine decided to do a little experiment. They brought several drivers to an airport runway in Michigan and let them each try driving through a series of tests. First they tested each of their normal reaction times; then they had them try reading texts and typing replies. As expected, the texting slowed down their reaction time significantly. The researchers measured exactly how many feet farther the car traveled before the brakes came on. At 35 miles per hour, one of the drivers rolled an extra 45 feet before braking (several car lengths). At 70 miles an hour, one driver rolled about 70 feet before hitting the brakes.

But here's where the test got really interesting. The researchers then served the drivers alcohol until each of them drank past their legal limit. Then they put them back in the car intoxicated and did the tests again.

The results?

Yes, their reaction time under the influence was worse than their normal reaction time. But all of the drivers were quicker to react while intoxicated than while texting. In fact, their "drunk" reaction time was six to eighteen times quicker than their "texting" reaction time.[8]

QUESTIONS TO PONDER

1. What do you think are some of the "urgent" tasks people want to do most while driving?
2. How urgent are these tasks if they risk killing someone?
3. What laws do you think would be helpful in regard to "messaging and driving"?
4. What do you think distracts you (or will distract you) the most while driving?
5. What can you do when you drive to avoid being distracted by your phone?

SOMETHING TO THINK ABOUT

It's all about being prepared.

So many distractions occur because we are trying to do something "on the run." We get in the car and then decide we want to pull up our favorite playlist, send a quick message to our friend, or read some quick details about where we're going.

You can do all these before you even take your foot off the brake pedal.

Make it a habit. Get in the car, put on your seatbelt, and then ask yourself, "Is there anything I'll need from my phone during this drive?" If so, do it right then before the vehicle moves an inch.

- Turn on my favorite playlist (one that won't tempt me to skip songs while driving).
- Text my friend and tell him I'll be there soon, but I'm driving and can't respond.
- Check the directions on my map app and make sure I know where I'm going.
- Then click my phone in its holder (you can buy really cool dash-mounts for your phone so you can see its GPS), push GO, and begin following the instructions from the smooth British voice telling me to turn left in 100 feet.

It's all about the prep—and it can save someone's life!

Tip #18

I see London, I see France.

Why are you showing your underpants?

S end nudes."

The phrase is joked about so much, it seems like sending naked pics is no big deal. Is it?

Ask Kelly.

Kelly was seventeen when she decided to send her boyfriend a picture of herself topless. After all, she'd been hearing that everybody was sending these kinds of pictures. So why not?

Sadly, the same thing happened to Kelly that has happened to hundreds of girls. The guy didn't turn out to be as trustworthy as she thought, and he decided to share her private little picture with others.

Months passed, and then one morning Kelly woke up to find that her phone was blowing up with texts from her friends. "There's a picture of you. You're wearing jeans and you're pulling your shirt up."

The picture had been picked up by a porn site featuring girls in her area. It posted her name and where she lived.

Kelly's life was never the same.

Word quickly spread around the school, and Kelly began to receive cruel texts and comments.

"They were laughing about it. I got really upset," Kelly explained. "I started crying my eyes out. I didn't want to go to school, I just wanted to quit. I don't know, it broke my heart."[1]

Kelly finally told her parents, and the police got involved.

What Kelly didn't know is that it was actually illegal even to share a naked picture of herself. Luckily for her, the police didn't go after her, but they began pursuing the people who were passing on the pics.

If you've read the other chapters in this book, you know that Kelly isn't the only girl who has regretted posted pics. Thousands upon thousands of girls have made that mistake. The story is always the same. Someone feels the pressure to send nudes, and they finally give in. Days, weeks, or even months pass, and then one day the picture shows up somewhere they never intended.

They always regret it.

And it's not just naked pics. People often regret the sexy "underwear" pics they post. Even a celeb like Kylie Jenner seems to have a little "post–post regret" after she posts a sexy pic.

"When I post sexy photos, I always regret it," she said.[2]

Apparently that doesn't run in the family. Her sister Kim Kardashian released a phone case with little hearts and the words "send nudes."[3]

That's what makes the situation even more difficult for young people today. Everybody is treating sending nude pictures like it's no big deal, but anyone who has experienced it realizes it actually is a huge deal. Especially those who have experienced jail time.

THE LAW

Yes, sending nudes is actually illegal in most states. Lawmakers have been arguing about it for years. Most young people don't realize this fact. Sexting is considered child pornography in most regions and carries a conviction of jail time and sex offender registration.[4]

Let's say sixteen-year-old Chris asks sixteen-year-old Brianna to send him nudes, and Brianna agrees. Then she is officially sending him a picture of a "minor." Authorities in most states deem that "child pornography."

If Chris decides to send those nudes to a bunch of his friends, Chris and Brianna both can be charged, but prosecutors in this case typically go after Chris because he is the one passing around the pic.

Most young people aren't aware of these rules. In fact, in a recent study. . .

- 61 percent of young people were not aware that sending nudes could be considered child pornography.
- 59 percent of young people reported that knowledge of legal consequences "would have" or "probably would have" deterred them from sending nudes.
- 71 percent of young people reported knowing other teens who experienced negative consequences after sending nudes.[5]

But let me ask you a bigger question. Is the threat of jail time really what's required to get us to stop passing around naked pictures?

Let's consider something else for a moment. Let's look forward to what we want in the future. Would you like to save sex for marriage, even if you've made some choices you regret in the past? Forget the past (God is willing to forget it—see Hebrews 8:12); what would you like from this point on?

Studies show that our attitude toward "sending nudes" is connected to our attitude about sex in general. Most research shows that teens who send sexy pics are significantly more likely to engage in sexual activity. Consider these stats:

- Of the girls who reported sending nudes, 77 percent also reported having sex.
- Of the girls who *did not* send nudes, only 42 percent reported having sex.
- Of the boys who reported sending nudes, 82 percent also reported having sex.
- Of the boys who did *not send* nudes, only 45 percent reported having sex.

And interestingly enough:

- Of the girls who said they weren't bothered by being asked to send nudes, 96 percent also reported having sex.
- Of the girls who said they were bothered by being asked to send nudes, only 45 percent reported having sex.[6]

God designed sexual activity to be enjoyed with one person for life. The simple fact is, when we flirt with others sensually and provoke them to think about us sexually, then sex is usually the result.

God's Word tells us to avoid any kind of situation that would tempt us to have sex before marriage.

I know this can be difficult in a culture where almost every message we see and hear is trying to convince us to "lose control" or "do what feels good at the moment" (something we already talked about in depth in the earlier chapter on our entertainment media choices). That's why I want to remind you how much God cares about you and wants you to value your own body. He cares about what you do to your body. In fact, if you have put your trust in Him, He calls your body His "temple."

Paul explains this in 1 Corinthians 6:18–20:

Run from sexual sin! No other sin so clearly affects the body as this one does. For sexual immorality is a sin against your own body. Don't you realize that your body is the temple of the Holy Spirit, who lives in you and was given to you by God? You do not belong to yourself, for God bought you with a high price. So you must honor God with your body.

When Paul uses the words "sexual sin" and "sexual immorality," he's using a word to describe when people decide to engage in sexual activity reserved only for marriage. Some people argue that he only means "intercourse"—nothing else. But scripture doesn't say that. In fact, if you need a reminder of what scripture actually says, I encourage you to reread the chapter in this book about pornography (Tip #4: "The Whole Picture of Those Pictures"). Because in that chapter we read Jesus' teaching on the subject, and He made the truth clear when He basically said, "If you are thinking sexual thoughts in regard to someone who is not your spouse, then you're committing adultery in your heart" (see Matthew 6:28).

Sending nudes always provokes sexual thoughts. Let's be honest. No one sends nudes so their boyfriend or girlfriend can study their body scientifically. People send nudes because it "turns on" the recipient. And that's the kind of activity God asks you to save until you've committed to the one you love in marriage.

QUESTIONS TO PONDER

1. Why do you think so many young people think sending nudes is "no big deal"?

2. What are some of the unforeseen consequences of a young teenager sending a nude picture of him- or herself?

3. Why do you think Paul warns us to run from sexual sin?

4. What are some examples of sexual sin? (Look back at Matthew 6:28 if you must.)

5. What are ways we can "run" from these kinds of temptations today?

6. What do you need to adjust in your world of technology and/or entertainment media to help you avoid these kinds of temptations? Explain.

SOMETHING TO THINK ABOUT

People can be really mean to those who get caught posting something they regret. It's easy to get entangled in gossiping about or teasing the person who messed up.

If you read through the New Testament in the Bible, you'll discover many stories where Jesus interacted with people who had really messed up in the past. He met men who had swindled money (Luke 19), for example, and women who had slept around (John 4), and in all of these situations. . .His reaction might surprise you.

Jesus never condemned these people for their past mistakes or foolish choices. It's almost as if He knew that they were well aware of their own sin. Instead, He just loved them, offering His forgiveness and a fresh start.

If you have put your trust in Jesus and follow Him, then I encourage you to imitate His attitude toward sinners. Here's what I mean. Chances are, you're going to encounter some people at your school or on your sports teams who mess up big-time. Ask yourself, "How would Jesus respond to this person?" He wouldn't celebrate their sin, but He wouldn't make them feel like an idiot either.

What if all of Christ's followers actually followed His advice to "do unto others" what we'd want others to do to us? (Having others heed this advice is especially nice when we're the one who messes up!)

This world is full of plenty of messed-up people. We probably should keep in mind that we are one of those messed-up people (Romans 3:23), and we need Jesus just as much as the next person.

Let's remember this if we ever meet someone who gets caught doing something raunchy or profane. You don't need to address it. You don't need to try to think of anything profound to say. Just show them love. Maybe sit and eat lunch with them. Invite them to hang out with you.

Who knows, they might even ask you, "Why are you being so nice to me?" And you can respond, "Jesus said, 'Do unto others what you want them to do to you.' I just figured that's the way I'd like to be treated."

Tip #19

No secrets.
The implications of "Finsta"

*A*llison and Trevor had become pretty close friends. They enjoyed the same music and quickly discovered they could talk about most anything. The two of them hung out at lunch most days and messaged each other throughout the evening.

Allison always hoped Trevor would like her as more than a friend, but she was too scared to say anything. So she just enjoyed the friendship, hoping maybe he would ask her out on a date.

The two actually went out together casually with a group of friends on several occasions. Allison's friends even pulled her aside and asked, "Are you guys going out?"

Allison always shrugged her shoulders. "We'll see."

One Sunday afternoon when they hadn't seen each other for a couple of days, the two of them were texting and Trevor commented, "Wow. I always have no problem opening up to you."

He had never texted anything like that before. Allison beamed! *Maybe he's interested.*

The two continued texting, and late in their conversation, Trevor made a random comment about *not* having a girlfriend. Allison explored. "What? I thought for sure you'd be interested in someone."

Trevor replied, "Waiting for someone special."

Allison took that as hopeful.

The next day Allison saw Trevor's good friends Nick and

Jackson at lunch. "Where's Trevor?" she asked.

"Probably with Christina," Nick said, laughing.

"They were making out all Friday night," Jackson added.

Nick teased Jackson. "You're just jealous that she wasn't with you."

Allison didn't reply as the two obliviously bantered back and forth. She felt sick to her stomach and scurried out of the lunchroom.

Allison didn't even know why she was upset. It wasn't as if Trevor was her boyfriend. They were just good friends. But Allison really had fallen for him, and this news was devastating.

Later that day Trevor passed her on the way to his class. "Hey, Alli! Missed you."

Allison was quiet.

Trevor didn't pick up on her somber mood. "What did you do this weekend?"

"Nothing," Allison said. "What about you?"

Trevor laughed. "Nothing. Just stayed home and played Xbox."

"Really?" Allison pressed. "A popular guy like you didn't have anywhere to hang on Friday night?"

"Nope," Trevor said, adjusting his backpack on his shoulder. "Well, I'd better get to class." And he continued on his way.

Allison went into the bathroom and bawled. She was mad at herself for reacting this way, but she was hurt on so many different levels. One, the guy she liked didn't seem to like her back as anything more than a "hallway conversation buddy." Second, he didn't think twice about lying to her. Even if they were just friends. . .why did he have to hide what happened with Christina?

Many of us have experienced situations like this. Maybe

not exactly like this, but circumstances where someone lied to us or held back information. Maybe it wasn't even a romantic interest, but just a friend who did something behind your back and tried to hide it from you.

It's funny. No matter how justified someone may seem in telling a lie. . .no matter how good of a reason they provide. . .it always still hurts!

More so, it destroys trust.

We feel betrayed.

No one enjoys feeling betrayed.

So why do so many young people have no problem betraying the trust of their parents?

HIDING IN PLAIN SIGHT

Earlier in this book, I encouraged you to "friend" Mom and Dad. Now I'm going to ask you to consider a strategy that will absolutely enhance your relationship with your parents. I call it "no secrets."

The notion is simple. You don't hide stuff from Mom and Dad, like creating a "Finstagram" account, for example.

As many of you know, Finstagram is just a term for "fake" Instagram.

Most young people claim that Finsta accounts are where they can be "real." But the reality is, a Finsta account is typically a place where someone can post the stuff they don't want most people to see. It's for "specific friends" only, certainly not anyone in authority like Mom or Dad. For some it's just a place to post silly photos or videos that they wouldn't necessarily post for "everyone." But let's be honest. For many young people, a Finsta account is where they feel free to cuss, be rude, or post content without fear of consequences.

Here are some thoughts to consider:

1. Whenever you create any account without your name on it, the lack of accountability tempts most people to behave in ways they wouldn't behave if Mom, Dad, or Boss were in the room. Just remember, many of these accounts get discovered, and then Mom, Dad, or Boss sees what you're really like. (Remember the chapter on the myth of anonymity—Tip #6: "Unmask"?)

2. Similarly, fake or anonymous accounts give you a false sense of freedom. They make you feel like you can post anything with no consequences. Sadly, most people find out the hard way this is nowhere close to being true. (Remember the chapter on thinking before you post—Tip #15: "Pause"?)

3. When you create an account without Mom or Dad's knowledge, you risk breaking their trust.

I know, it's difficult being honest in a world where 59 percent of teenagers have hidden, edited, or deleted posts on social media to prevent their parents from seeing what they've posted.[1] Statistically, that means six out of ten of your friends don't mind hiding stuff from their parents.

Maybe you should consider hanging out with the other four.

Funny how the whole purpose of social media is to be "social". . .yet many people don't put much thought into who they are really spending time with online and how their behavior changes when they hang with these online friends.

I can't help but think of King David literally thousands of years ago, because his words on this subject still ring true today, even in the world of social media. He said this about the people he chose to surround himself with:

> *I will search for faithful people to be my companions. Only those who are above reproach will be allowed to serve me. I will not allow deceivers to serve in my house, and liars will not stay in my presence.* (Psalm 101:6–7)

Wow. David took honesty seriously.

I don't need to go into greater detail about this subject, because at this point in the book we've covered it. You know that anonymous sites aren't truly anonymous. And people who think they can hide their posts are often gravely disappointed.

So let me simply ask you this: When is it ever worth it to try to hide something from your parents?

QUESTIONS TO PONDER

1. Have you ever had someone lie to you or do something behind your back like in the story of Allison and Trevor?
2. Why do the majority of young people have no problem hiding things from their parents?
3. David uses several different terms to describe honest people. What does each of those terms mean?
4. How can we be faithful to our friends?
5. How can we be faithful to our parents?
6. What might you need to change about your social media habits?

SOMETHING TO THINK ABOUT

In the previous chapter we read a story about a teenage girl who trusted her boyfriend so much she made a foolish decision. She chose to send him a nude picture.

Yes, that decision was unwise. But consider something else for a moment. What kind of guy would take something so private, so entrusted. . .and pass it around to friends?

This story probably angered many of you. Even though this girl's decision to send him a nude picture was a mistake on many levels, it was still extremely cruel of her boyfriend to break her trust and send it to his friends.

Inexcusable.

It's no fun being betrayed.

It hurts when someone breaks our trust.

Do I even have to say it?

Tip #20

Sleep matters.
Saying "nighty night" to distractions

$\mathcal{D}$o you get enough sleep each night?

What if I asked you that question when your alarm was going off on a school morning?

"Wakey, wakey! Or would you like to sleep longer?"

Most teenagers feel they don't get enough sleep.

And they're right! Experts agree. A study by the National Sleep Foundation revealed the average amount of sleep teenagers get each night is about seven and a half hours. For older teenagers the average is closer to seven hours.[1] That's about two hours short per night of the nine hours and fifteen minutes recommended by experts. So by the end of the week, teenagers are short on what adds up to almost two nights of sleep. Maybe that's why the American Academy of Pediatrics actually called the problem of tired teenagers "a public health epidemic."[2]

And guess what?

Technology is only making the problem worse.

Don't hate me for showing you the studies, but experts have launched recent reports warning parents, "Children who leave electronic devices on at night get less sleep on school nights than other children do." In fact, "teens who leave devices on are estimated to get, on average, half an hour less sleep on school nights" (which is pretty rough, when you're already two hours short each night).[3] This report isn't alone in its findings. A study in the medical journal *Pediatrics* found that "taking a phone into the bedroom led to longer sleep latency, worse sleep quality, more sleep disturbance, and more daytime dysfunction."[4]

Maybe some of you are thinking, *So what! What's the big deal if I'm tired the next day?*

GRADES

I guess this sleep shortage wouldn't be such a big deal if the only consequence were feeling grumpy. Sadly, every expert out there is showing a connection between sleep loss and bad grades. It's not hard to believe. I know when I'm sleep deprived I find it almost impossible to read or study. And that's exactly what these studies reveal. In fact, one researcher described sleep deprivation as having the same effect on students' grades as binge drinking and marijuana use.[5]

If you're awake enough to do math, try out these equations:

Bedroom + technology = less sleep

Less sleep = bad grades

I don't want to beat a dead horse. . .but there's more.

Social media is making the problem even worse.

In past chapters we examined some of the effects of social media on the brain. Young people who spend considerable hours on social media daily actually become almost addicted to it. So it's probably not surprising to you that studies now show it's difficult to "shut off" social media browsing come sleep time.

A brand-new study from across the pond has revealed that one out of five kids wakes up regularly at night to check social media.[6] This isn't the first major sleep study of its kind, but it is unique to find so many young people actually waking up to see if they got more "likes" on the pic they just posted of their cat wearing mittens. Other studies show the "mere presence of devices" in the room affected sleep, *even if switched off*.[7] They blame the effect of social media on the brain—young people are used to being continually stimulated by devices.

Enough of these studies! (I'm afraid if I share any more, I'm going to put you to sleep!)

The question each of us needs to ask is, "How can I enjoy my technology without hurting myself in the long run?"

UNDISTRACTED ENVIRONMENT

Forget all these studies for a moment. Consider these questions honestly:

1. Do you tend to get a little more amped up or excited if you use technology right before bed?
2. Do you have a hard time "calling it quits" and putting down your device when it's time to go to bed?
3. If you keep your phone near your bed, do you find yourself picking it up to check for messages once the lights are out?
4. Have you found yourself wandering into online locations or chatting situations you wouldn't visit if you weren't alone in your bedroom late at night?

If you answered "yes" to any of these questions, you're not alone. A lot of people struggle with these distractions. Frankly, a lot of *adults* struggle with them. It takes discipline to create an environment where you aren't distracted by your own technology.

This kind of discipline is called self-discipline, and it means exactly what it implies. It means it's up to you if you'd like to be successful in this area. For many of you, your parents don't enforce a lot of rules regarding the use of your phone. I know, because I teach parent workshops frequently and find that most parents ignore the advice from their doctor to "keep devices out of the bedroom" (something experts have been recommending for years now).[8] So it's really up to you to show restraint in this area.

And even if your parents do restrict your use of devices in the bedroom *now*, someday soon you'll be in a college dorm, a military barracks, or your own apartment, and you will be the only one who makes these decisions for yourself.

What will you decide?

Here are two considerations:

1. *Power down devices and/or stick them in a charger away from your bed at night.*

   Enjoy your devices during the day. Then come bedtime, turn off your phone and put it somewhere out of the room or out of reach for the night. Many of us need this discipline to keep our phone from distracting us. If you need to leave your device on for backup purposes, that's okay. Just make sure it's somewhere you won't hear it vibrate and you won't be tempted to "just check something really quick."

2. *Time yourself.*

   If you're one of the rare people who can keep your device on and within reach of your pillow without it distracting you (if you can honestly answer "no" to all four of the questions I asked above), then you may want to at least monitor the time you're spending on your device before bedtime. Thirty minutes seems to be the magic number. A recent study out of Rutgers looked at the link between nighttime instant messaging and school performance the next day. The researchers concluded, "Students who turned off their devices or who messaged for less than thirty minutes after lights out performed significantly better in school than those who messaged for more than thirty minutes after lights out."[9] The study showed a huge difference between students who limited their nighttime messaging and those who found themselves on their devices well into the night.

How much do you value your sleep?

QUESTIONS TO PONDER
1. Do you think you get enough sleep at night? Why or why not?
2. Why do you think people with devices get less sleep than people without?
3. Why do you think social media makes the problem even worse?
4. Have you found devices distracting to you come bedtime? How so?
5. What is a good way to keep your devices from distracting you from sleep?
6. What is something you can do this week to make that happen?

SOMETHING TO THINK ABOUT

Remember all the stories I've shared in this book so far—instances of young people posting pics they soon regretted, making comments they wish they could take back, or connecting with people who turned out to be vindictive or dangerous? I interact with young people and parents in these situations regularly. You'd be surprised how common they all are.

And do you know when most of these mistakes were made? *At night.*

I'm not saying people never make mistakes during the day. Sadly, humans make mistakes at all hours. But at night people are tired and alone, and those factors can trigger strong emotions. Add in the privacy of a bedroom with no accountability, and it's a bad mix altogether.

Do you *really* need your phone by your bedside?

Tip #21

Look up.
Staying aware of your surroundings

Standing right by a train ahaha this is awesome!!!!"

The last words Savannah ever typed, accompanied by a horrifying photo. . .the last photo she ever took.

The photo shows Savannah, her sister Kelsea, and their friend Essa all posing for a train track selfie as a train passed by on a nearby track, blowing their hair back. What they didn't notice was captured in the background of their disturbing photo—the headlight of an oncoming train in the distance behind them.

They never saw it coming.

The approaching train was far enough off that Savannah even had time to post the photo. But the girls were oblivious to their surroundings, distracted by their phones, and deafened by the sound of the passing train.

The conductor and engineer of the oncoming train both clearly saw the girls in the tracks ahead of them, but trains can't "swerve" out of the way. And it can take more than a mile to stop a train at full speed. The two train operators blared their horn and futilely screamed at the girls, but the three couldn't hear a thing.

"They were in their own little world," recalled the conductor.

The train struck the girls at 39 miles per hour. Kelsea and Essa were killed instantly, but Savannah survived the initial impact.

The train finally came to a complete stop a quarter of a mile down the tracks. The conductor hopped off the train and ran back, finding Savannah "clinging to life." He held her hand until the paramedics arrived.

"I told her everything would be okay, and she relaxed a little," the conductor recounted.

Savannah died three days later with internal bleeding, blood clots, and a severe brain injury.[1]

OBLIVIOUS

As technology has increased, our attentiveness to our surroundings has decreased. That little device is not only rarely in our pocket but is often distracting us from fundamental day-to-day skills. . .like driving or walking down the street!

We've already read several stories in this book of people negligently killing others because they couldn't resist being on their phone. It makes sense that messaging would make it difficult to operate a vehicle. Apparently it distracts us from more than that.

A woman walking in China was routinely crossing the street, so engrossed in her phone she didn't even notice oncoming traffic. A slow-moving truck struck her in one lane, merely knocking her down, but giving her no time to jump clear of an oncoming truck in the other lane, which ran her over with its front and back wheels before coming to a stop.[2]

A San Diego man was walking along some beachside cliffs to take selfies. As he walked along, he paid more attention to his phone than the trail in front of him, and walked right off a sixty-foot cliff. Bystanders heard him scream on the way down. He was killed at the scene.[3]

The same year a woman took three of her young children

down to her apartment complex's pool area to let them play. I don't know what's more surprising, the fact that she knew the three of them couldn't swim, or the fact that she was so engrossed in her phone that she didn't even see them drowning. Witnesses who walked by the pool moments before said the mother was staring at her phone and oblivious of her children playing by the pool.[4]

Sadly, I could tell you hundreds of these stories.

Why?

People are so absorbed in their phones, they're oblivious to everything else around them.

The cure is simple.

"Look up."

I'll echo what I said in the beginning of this book: Your phone is *not* the problem. The problem is when we let our phone captivate us so significantly with the *unimportant* that we ignore the *important* all around us.

Most people are learning this the hard way. Take a look around next time you're walking down a busy sidewalk. Notice how many people are staring at their phones instead of their surroundings. They could be the next sad story in the evening news.

Just look up.

There is far more to life than what is on that tiny screen.

THE IMPORTANT

We are all familiar with distractions, literally and metaphorically. Staring at our phone while walking through traffic could truly cost us our life. But many of us let our phones distract us spiritually from our relationship with God. . .and that has an eternal price.

Why would we let *unimportant* things distract us from what's truly *important* in life?

As I wrap up this final chapter of the book, I want to remind you one last time to "look up," not just to your physical surroundings but to your Creator, trusting Him to guide you as you seek to live out His wisdom each day.

You've heard a lot of truth in this book, the most important being the wisdom from God's Word. So I encourage you, as a young man or woman, in the same way the apostle Paul encouraged a young man he was mentoring named Timothy:

> *But you must remain faithful to the things you have been taught. You know they are true, for you know you can trust those who taught you. You have been taught the holy Scriptures from childhood, and they have given you the wisdom to receive the salvation that comes by trusting in Christ Jesus. All Scripture is inspired by God and is useful to teach us what is true and to make us realize what is wrong in our lives. It corrects us when we are wrong and teaches us to do what is right. God uses it to prepare and equip his people to do every good work.* (2 Timothy 3:14–17)

If Paul were mentoring you today, he'd probably tell you the exact same thing. He'd tell you to *trust* the wisdom you've been taught. Be faithful to what you have learned.

Why does he even need to remind us of this?

Why does this take "faith" or "trust"?

Because life is so full of distractions that we sometimes choose temporary pleasures over what we know is best for us in the long run. Think about that statement. Why would someone choose quick thrills at the cost of long-term fulfillment?

It's all about our focus. Are you focusing on what's immediately in front of you. . .or the bigger picture? No, I'm not talking about your phone. I'm asking you, are you so focused on today that you're neglecting tomorrow?

It takes faith to remember what you were taught, recognize its truth, and apply it daily in the midst of distractions.

Where is your focus?

QUESTIONS TO PONDER

1. Share a time you've witnessed someone so distracted with their device, they had no clue what was going on around them. (I don't think it will be difficult to think of an example.)

2. Share a time when you were similarly distracted by your device.

3. What is a good way to keep your phone from distracting you from your physical surroundings in situations like these?

4. Where are some places you might need to practice "looking up"?

5. In the Bible passage I shared from 2 Timothy, Paul said the scriptures he was taught gave him wisdom. Name one piece of wisdom that impacted you from the scriptures you read in the pages of this book.

6. What is one area of your life where you need to let scripture correct you and "teach [you] to do what is right"?

7. What will that look like in your life this week?

SOMETHING TO THINK ABOUT

Read that 2 Timothy passage again. Then pray and ask God to help you apply what you read. Here are some things you might ask Him:

- Help me remain faithful to what I've been taught.
- Equip me to recognize lies that distract me from the truth.
- Encourage me to stay in Your Word.
- Teach me to do what is right.

Then get up, put your phone in your back pocket, and look around you. Wander outside, look up, and take it all in. Walk into a room with the people you care about, look them in the eyes, and begin a conversation.

And when you sit down by yourself later, pull out your phone and post something you observed or a piece of wisdom you gathered.

Message a friend.

Make a playlist.

Watch something fun.

Read something inspiring.

And when it's bedtime, set your phone on the charger somewhere out of sight. . .and get a good night's sleep!

Notes

A Note to Mom or Dad Screening This Book

1. "The Common Sense Census: Media Use by Tweens and Teens," Common Sense Media, 2015, https://www.commonsensemedia.org/sites/default/files/uploads/research/census_executivesummary.pdf.

2. Michael Robb, "Common Sense Media Census Measures Plugged-in Parents," Common Sense Media, December 5, 2016, https://www.commonsensemedia.org/blog/common-sense-media-census-measures-plugged-in-parents.

3. "Children's Online Privacy Protection Act," http://www.coppa.org.

4. Cris Rowan, "Ten Reasons Why Handheld Devices Should Be Banned for Children under the Age of Twelve," *Huffington Post*, March 6, 2014, http://www.huffingtonpost.com/cris-rowan/10-reasons-why-handheld-devices-should-be-banned_b_4899218.html.

5. Victor C. Strasburger and Marjorie J. Hogan, "Children, Adolescents, and the Media," *Pediatrics* 132, no. 5 (November 2013), http://pediatrics.aappublications.org/content/132/5/958.

6. Ibid.

7. "Children and Media—Tips for Parents," American Academy of Pediatrics, 2015, https://www.aap.org/en-us/about-the-aap/aap-press-room/Pages/Children-And-Media-Tips-For-Parents.aspx.

A Note to You

1. Bill Chappell, "2015 Traffic Fatalities Rose by Largest Percent in 50 Years, Safety Group Says," *The Two-Way*, February 18, 2016, http://www.npr.org/sections/thetwo-way/2016/02/18/467230965/2015-traffic-fatalities-rose-by-largest-percent-in-50-years-safety-group-says.

2. "Adolescent Health," Centers for Disease Control and Prevention, National Center for Health Statistics, March 31, 2017, http://www.cdc.gov/nchs/fastats/adolescent-health.htm.

3. "Teen Drivers: Get the Facts," Centers for Disease Control and Prevention, Motor Vehicle Safety, April 20, 2017, http://www.cdc.gov/motorvehiclesafety/teen_drivers/teendrivers_factsheet.html.

4. "Dealing with Devices: The Parent-Teen Dynamic," Common Sense Media, May 3, 2016, https://www.commonsensemedia.org/technology-addiction-concern-controversy-and-finding-balance-infographic.

5. Ibid.

6. Elliot Rosenhaus, "10 Horrific Deaths Caused by Cell Phones," Listverse, http://listverse.com/2016/03/25/10-horrific-deaths-caused-by-smartphones/.

7. Andrew K. Przybylski and Netta Weinstein, "Can You Connect with Me Now?" *Journal of Social and Personal Relationships* 30, no. 3 (2013), http://spr.sagepub.com/content/early/2012/07/17/0265407512453827.abstract.

8. Shalini Misra, Lulu Cheng, Jamie Genevie, and Miao Yuan, "The iPhone Effect," *Environment and Behavior* 48, no. 2 (February 2016), http://eab.sagepub .com/content/early/2014/05/31/0013916514539755 .abstract.

9. Jimi Hendrix, BrainyQuote, https://www.brainyquote .com/quotes/quotes/j/jimihendri103615.html?src=t_ wisdom.

10. Aristotle, Goodreads, http://www.goodreads.com/ quotes/tag/wisdom.

Tip #1: Love the one you're with.

1. Amanda Lenhart, "Mobile Access Shifts Social Media Use and Other Online Activities," Pew Research Center, April 9, 2015, http://www.pewinternet.org/2015/04/09/mobile-access-shifts-social-media-use-and-other-online-activities/.

2. Yalda T. Uhls, Minas Michikyan, Jordan Morris, et al. "Five Days at Outdoor Education Camp without Screens Improves Preteen Skills with Nonverbal Emotion Cues," *Computers in Human Behavior* 39 (October 2014): 387–92, http://www.sciencedirect.com/science/article/pii/S0747563214003227.

3. Lauren E. Sherman, Minas Michikyan, and Patricia M. Greenfield, "The Effects of Text, Audio, Video, and In-Person Communication on Bonding between Friends", *Cyberpsychology* 7 (no. 2), 2013, http://www.cyberpsychology.eu/view.php?cisloclanku=2013071101&article=3.

4. Sherry Turkle, "Stop Googling. Let's Talk," *New York Times*, September 26, 2015, http://www.nytimes.com/2015/09/27/opinion/sunday/stop-googling-lets-talk.html?_r=1.

5. Pauline Dakin, "Social Media Affecting Teens' Concepts of Friendship, Intimacy," CBC News, February 24, 2014, http://www.cbc.ca/news/health/social-media-affecting-teens-concepts-of-friendship-intimacy-1.2543158.

6. Turkle, "Stop Googling."

Tip #2: Peek at your privacy settings.

1. Safer Roads, http://www.saferroads.org/advice/drivers/seatbelts/.
2. Joseph Serna, "Man Allegedly Used Facebook, Instagram to Find Women, Steal Their Underwear," *Los Angeles Times*, December 8, 2015, http://www.latimes.com/local/lanow/la-me-ln-social-media-undergarment-thief-20151208-story.html.

Tip #3: Nothing you post is temporary.

1. Radhika Sanghani, "Revenge Porn: Why Teen Girls Aren't Shocked to Find Their Nude Selfies Shared at School," *The Telegraph*, October 12, 2015, http://www.telegraph.co.uk/women/womens-life/11926455/Revenge-porn-Teen-girls-arent-surprised-by-nude-selfies-being-shared.html.
2. "2014 Social Recruiting Survey," Jobvite, http://timedotcom.files.wordpress.com/2014/09/jobvite_socialrecruiting_survey2014.pdf.
3. Ibid.

Tip #4: The whole picture of those pictures.

1. Nisha Lilia Diu, "How Porn Is Rewiring Our Brains," *The Telegraph*, November 15, 2013, http://www.telegraph.co.uk/men/thinking-man/10441027/How-porn-is-rewiring-our-brains.html.
2. Denali Tietjen, "Men Who Watch Pornography Have Small Brains," Boston.com, May 30, 2014, https://www.boston.com/culture/health/2014/05/30/men-who-watch-pornography-have-small-brains.

3. Belinda Luscombe, "Porn: Why Young Men Who Grew Up with Internet Porn Are Becoming Advocates for Turning It Off," *Time Magazine*, April 11, 2016, http://time.com/4277510/porn-and-the-threat-to-virility/.

4. Ibid.

5. Ibid.

6. Christina Cauterucci, "Why Are More and More Teen Girls Getting Cosmetic Genital Surgery?" *Slate*, April 26, 2016, http://www.slate.com/blogs/xx_factor/2016/04/26/why_is_cosmetic_genital_surgery_on_the_rise_among_teen_girls.html.

7. Jonathan McKee, "The Limp Truth about Porn," *Jonathan's Blog*, April 18, 2016, http://www.jonathanmckeewrites.com/archive/2016/04/18/limp-truth-porn.aspx.

8. Julie Ruvolo, "How Much of the Internet Is Actually for Porn," *Forbes*, September 7, 2011, http://www.forbes.com/sites/julieruvolo/2011/09/07/how-much-of-the-internet-is-actually-for-porn/#6e698bef61f7.

10. Jonathan McKee, *Sex Matters* (Minneapolis: Bethany House, 2015).

Tip #5: Don't do this alone.

1. Angela Bronner Helm, "Watch: Allen Iverson's Epic Hall of Fame Speech Left Nary a Dry Eye in the House," *The Root*, September 10, 2016, http://www.theroot.com/articles/news/2016/09/watch-allen-iversons-epic-hall-of-fame-speech/.

2. Swati Arora, "Famous Mentors and Their Famous Mentees," *Mentorpolis*, October 15, 2012, http://www

.mentorpolis.com/famous-mentors-and-their-fa-
mous-mentees/; Tory Hoen, "9 Famous Men-
tor-Mentee Duos You Should Meet," *The M Dash*,
https://mmlafleur.com/mdash/9-famous-mentor
mentee-duos; DesignMentoring, "Interesting Pairs
of Famous Mentors-Mentees in History," *Over My
Shoulder Foundation* blog, May 13, 2014, http://over
myshoulderfoundation.org/interesting-pairs-of
-famous-mentors-mentees-in-history/; Jean Rhodes,
"Top 25 Mentoring Relationships in History,"
Chronicle of Evidence-Based Mentoring, September 13, 2015, http://chronicle.umbmentoring.org/
top-25-mentoring-relationships-in-history/.

3. Drew Appleby, quoted in Heather Stringer, "The
Life-Changing Power of Mentors," *Monitor on Psychology* 47, no. 6 (June 2016): 54; http://www.apa.org/
monitor/2016/06/mentors.aspx.

Tip #6: Unmask.

1. Natasha Stokes, "The Worst Apps for Privacy," Tech-
licious, December 18, 2014, http://www.techlicious
.com/tip/the-worst-apps-for-privacy/.

2. Paul Lewis and Dominic Rushe, "Revealed: How
Whisper App Tracks 'Anonymous' Users," *Guardian*,
October 16, 2014, https://www.theguardian.com/
world/2014/oct/16/-sp-revealed-whisper-app-track
ing-users.

3. Moriah Balingit, "Millions of Teens Are Using a
New App to Post Anonymous Thoughts, and Most
Parents Have No Idea," *Washington Post*, December
8, 2015, https://www.washingtonpost.com/local/

education/millions-of-teens-are-using-a-new-app-to-post-anonymous-thoughts-and-most-parents-have-no-idea/2015/12/08/1532a98c-9907-11e5-8917-653b65c809eb_story.html?utm_term=.bc16ca9cb7c6.

4. Cecilia Kang, "Seeking Privacy, Teens Turn to Anonymous-Messaging Apps," *Washington Post*, February 16, 2014, https://www.washingtonpost.com/business/technology/seeking-privacy-teens-turn-to-anonymous-messaging-apps/2014/02/16/1ffa583a-9362-11e3-b46a-5a3d0d2130da_story.html.

5. Balingit, "Millions of Teens Are Using a New App."

Tip #7: Yes, still don't talk with strangers.

1. *Dr. Phil Show*, "How Social Media May Have Played Role in Death of 13-Year-Old Nicole Lovell," *Huffington Post*, February 10, 2016, http://www.huffingtonpost.com/entry/nicole-lovell-death-social-media_us_56bae980e4b0c3c5504f6f24.

2. Jackie Bensen, "D.C. Police: Teen Killed by Man Met on Social Networking Site," NBC News, January 29, 2013, http://www.nbcwashington.com/news/local/DC-Police-Teen-Killed-by-Man-Met-on-Social-Networking-Site-188926201.html.

3. Jason Kandel, "Man Arrested after Befriending Girl on Social Media Dating Site," NBC News, November 16, 2014, http://www.nbclosangeles.com/news/local/Man-Arrested-After-Befriending-Girl-on-Social-Media-Dating-Site-400330941.html.

4. "Aurora Man Arrested Following Social Media Correspondence," World-Herald News Service, November 2, 2016, http://lexch.com/news/aurora-man-arrested-

following-social-media-correspondence/arti
cle_4b82a1a8-a10e-11e6-bddf-e3f042261ca7.html.

5. Christie Martin, "Man Arrested for Soliciting Boys Met on Social Media for Sex," 24/7 Headline News, August 4, 2016, https://247headline.com/man-arrest ed-for-soliciting-boys-met-on-social-media-for-sex/.

6. Amanda Lenhart, "Teens, Technology and Friendships," Pew Research Center, August 6, 2015, http:// www.pewinternet.org/2015/08/06/teens-technolo gy-and-friendships/.

7. Charlene Aaron, "Perfect Stranger: How Social Media Led to Her Daughter's Death," CBN News, April 15, 2016, http://www1.cbn.com/cbnnews/us/2015/Octo ber/Grieving-Mother-Warns-of-Online-Predators.

Tip #8: Take more "seflessies."

1. Julia Glum, "Millennials Selfies: Young Adults Will Take More Than 25,000 Pictures of Themselves during Their Lifetimes," *International Business Times*, September 22, 2015, http://www.ibtimes.com/millen nials-selfies-young-adults-will-take-more-25000-pic tures-themselves-during-2108417.

2. Chris Gayomali, "10 Rules for Taking #Selfies on Instagram," *The Week*, January 31, 2013, http://theweek .com/articles/468106/5-rules-taking-selfies-instagram.

3. Haley Bloomingdale, "Instagram Rules: The Good, the Bad, and the Very Boring," *Vogue*, August 26, 2015, http://www.vogue.com/13299678/insta gram-rules-social-media/.

4. Mahita Gajanan, "Young Women on Instagram and Self-Esteem: 'I Absolutely Feel Insecure,' " *Guardian*,

November 4, 2015, https://www.theguardian.com/media/2015/nov/04/instagram-young-women-self-esteem-essena-oneill.

5. Ibid.

Tip #9: Like me!

1. Susie East, "Teens: This Is How Social Media Affects Your Brain," CNN, August 1, 2016, http://www.cnn.com/2016/07/12/health/social-media-brain/.

2. Judith E. Glaser, "Science Explains the Millennial Brain," *Entrepreneur*, October 19, 2015, https://www.entrepreneur.com/article/251759.

3. "Drugs, Brains, and Behavior: The Science of Addiction," National Institute on Drug Abuse, July 2014, https://www.drugabuse.gov/publications/drugs-brains-behavior-science-addiction/drugs-brain.

4. Saul McLeod, "Skinner—Operant Conditioning," *Simply Psychology*, 2015, http://www.simplypsychology.org/operant-conditioning.html.

5. Kayleigh Lewis, "Heavy Social Media Users 'Trapped in Endless Cycle of Depression,'" *The Independent*, March 24, 2016, http://www.independent.co.uk/life-style/health-and-families/health-news/social-media-depression-facebook-twitter-health-young-study-a6948401.html.

Tip #10: Know the app before you snap.

1. Maya Kosoff, "Dozens of Teenagers Told Us What's Cool in 2016—These Are Their Favorite (and Least Favorite) Apps," *Business Insider*, January 31, 2016, http://www.businessinsider.com/teens-favorite-apps-

in-2016-2016-1/#what-are-teens-favorite-apps-here-are-a-few-of-the-most-popular-answers-2.

2. Jim Edwards, "Photos, Texts, and Emails Show the Alleged Betrayal at the Heart of Snapchat," *Business Insider*, August 11, 2013, http://www.businessinsider.com/snapchat-lawsuit-photos-texts-and-emails-2013-8.

3. "Snapchat Settles FTC Charges That Promises of Disappearing Messages Were False," Federal Trade Commission press release, May 8, 2014, https://www.ftc.gov/news-events/press-releases/2014/05/snapchat-settles-ftc-charges-promises-disappearing-messages-were.

4. Alyson Shontell, "Actually, Snapchat Doesn't Delete Your Private Pictures and Someone Found a Way to Resurface Them," *Business Insider*, May 9, 2013, http://www.businessinsider.com/snapchat-doesnt-delete-your-private-pictures-2013-5.

5. "The Easiest Way to Recover and View Snapchat Photos," Aiseesoft, http://www.aiseesoft.com/how-to/recover-snapchat-photos.html.

6. Federal Trade Commission complaint against Snapchat, Inc., 2014, https://www.ftc.gov/system/files/documents/cases/140508snapchatcmpt.pdf.

7. Ryan Gallagher, "Watch Your Naked Selfies: Snapchat Can Turn Photos Over to Government," Future Tense, October 15, 2013, http://www.slate.com/blogs/future_tense/2013/10/15/snapchat_reveals_it_sometimes_hands_over_photos_to_the_government.html.

Tip #11: Reevaluate your screen time.

1. "The Common Sense Census: Media Use by Tweens and Teens," Common Sense, 2015, https://www.commonsensemedia.org/sites/default/files/uploads/research/census_executivesummary.pdf.

2. Grant Tomkinson, "When It Comes to Fitness, US Kids Are at Back of Pack," *The Conversation*, October 13, 2016, http://www.cnn.com/2016/10/13/health/united-states-children-aerobic-fitness/.

3. American Academy of Pediatrics, "Children, Adolescents, and the Media," *Pediatrics* 132, no. 5 (November 2013), http://pediatrics.aappublications.org/content/132/5/958.full.

Tip #12: Frequent tech-free zones.

1. Brenda Breslauer, "What Happened When 9 Teens Gave Up Their Cellphones for a Week," *Today*, December 2, 2016, http://www.today.com/parents/9-teens-gave-their-phones-week-here-s-what-happened-t105539.

Tip #13: Friend Mom or Dad.

1. Shaunti Feldhahn, "2 Things to Do If You Want Your Teen to Talk to You," Shaunti Feldhahn: Research, Insight, Hope, June 29, 2016, http://www.shaunti.com/2016/06/2-things-to-do-if-you-want-your-teen-to-talk-to-you/.

2. KJ Dell'Antonia, "Don't Post about Me on Social Media, Children Say," *New York Times*, March 8, 2016, http://well.blogs.nytimes.com/2016/03/08/dont-post-

about-me-on-social-media-children-say/?_r=4.

3. McAfee, "America's Youth Admit to Surprising On-line Behavior, Would Change Actions If Parents Were Watching," McAfee press release, June 4, 2013, http://www.mcafee.com/us/about/news/2013/q2/20130604-01.aspx.

Tip #14: Dissect your entertainment media.

1. Susan Seligson, "Music Boosts Memory in Alzheimer's," *BU Today*, June 15, 2010, https://www.bu.edu/today/2010/music-boosts-memory-in-alzheimer%E2%80%99s/.

2. Chrysalis L. Wright and Michelle Craske, "Music's Influence on Risky Sexual Behaviors: Examining the Cultivation Theory," *Media Psychology Review* 9, no. 1 (2015), http://mprcenter.org/review/musics-influence-on-risky-sexual-behaviors-examining-the-cultivation-theory/.

3. "Dirty Song Lyrics Can Prompt Early Teen Sex," Associated Press, August 7, 2006, http://www.nbcnews.com/id/14227775/ns/health-sexual_health/t/dirty-song-lyrics-can-prompt-early-teen-sex/#.WIEF1pIlrvs.

4. Wright and Craske, "Music's Influence."

5. Ibid.

6. Ibid.

7. Centers for Disease Control and Prevention, "Reported STDs at Unprecedented High in the U.S.," 2015 STD Surveillance Report press release, October 19, 2016, http://www.cdc.gov/nchhstp/newsroom/2016/std-surveillance-report-2015-press-release.html.

8. Mary-Signe Chojnacki, Christina Grant, Kathryn Maguire, and Katie Regan, "Depleting Body Image: The Effects of Female Magazine Models on the Self-Esteem and Body Image of College-Age Women," research paper, University of Wisconsin–Madison, https://www.ssc.wisc.edu/~jpiliavi/357/body-image.htm.

9. American Psychological Association, "Report of the APA Task Force on the Sexualization of Girls," 2007, http://www.apa.org/pi/women/programs/girls/report.aspx.

10. "Lady Gaga Lands in London," Celebrity-Gossip.net, April 15, 2009, http://www.celebrity-gossip.net/celebrities/hollywood/lady-gaga-lands-in-london-212810.

11. *Mean Girls*, directed by Mark Waters, written by Tina Fey (Paramount, 2004), DVD.

12. American Psychological Association, "Report of the APA Task Force on the Sexualization of Girls."

Tip #15: Pause.

1. Craig Malisow, "A Young Man's Violent Threat on Facebook Lands Him in Jail, and Limbo," *Houston Press*, February 12, 2014, http://www.houstonpress.com/news/a-young-mans-violent-threat-on-facebook-lands-him-in-jail-and-limbo-6600703.

2. Claire Ricke, "New Braunfels Teen in Court for Threatening to Shoot Up a Kindergarten," KXAN, March 17, 2016, http://kxan.com/2016/03/17/new-braunfels-teen-in-court-for-threatening-to-shoot-up-a-kindergarten/.

3. "Teen Arrested for Making Clown-Related Threat

against Houston School," *ABC13* (Houston), October 3, 2016, http://abc13.com/news/houston-teen-ar rested-for-making-clown-threat/1537334/.

4. Caroline Schaeffer, "NYC Teen Charged with Terroristic Threats and Harassment after He Wrote a Facebook Post Using. . .Emojis," *Independent Journal Review*, April 9, 2015, http://ijr.com/2015/01/240303-nyc-teens-terroristic-use-emojis-facebook-ends-arrest-threats-harassment/.

5. Selma Abdelaziz, "Teen Arrested for Tweeting Airline Terror Threat," *CNN*, April 14, 2014, http://edition.cnn.com/2014/04/14/travel/dutch-teen-arrest-ameri can-airlines-terror-threat-tweet/.

6. Shane Paul Neil, "More Than Half of Americans Have Social Media Regrets," *Huffington Post*, July 27, 2016, http://www.huffingtonpost.com/shane-paul-neil/more-than-half-of-america_b_7872514.html.

7. Robert Kovacik and Sean Browning, "Teens Arrested in Connection with Clown Terror Threats to Schools," *NBC Los Angeles*, October 6, 2016, http://www.nbclosangeles.com/on-air/as-seen-on/19-Year-Old-Arrested-After-Clown-Threats-Against-School_Los-Angeles-396113261.html.

8. Ibid.

9. Ibid.

Tip #16: Crush criticism and cruelty.

1. Rebecca Hawkes, "Whatever Happened to Star Wars Kid? The Sad but Inspiring Story behind One of the First Victims of Cyberbullying," *The Telegraph*, May 4, 2016, http://www.telegraph.co.uk/films/2016/05/04/

whatever-happened-to-star-wars-kid-the-true-story-behind-one-of/.

2. Ibid.

3. Dove, "Dove Selfie: Redefining Beauty One Photo at a Time," posted on YouTube January 19, 2014, https://www.youtube.com/watch?v=BFkm1Hg4dTI.

4. Jeff Roberts, "Fake Boyfriend Shows (Again) Why We're Stuck with Online Cruelty," Gigaom, June 2, 2012, https://gigaom.com/2012/06/02/fake-boy friend-case-shows-again-why-were-stuck-with-on line-cruelty/.

5. William M. Bukowski, Brett Laursen, and Betsy Hoza, "The Snowball Effect: Friendship Moderates Escalations in Depressed Affect among Avoidant and Excluded Children," *Development and Psychopathology* 22, no. 4 (November 2010): 747–57; https://www.cambridge.org/core/jour nals/development-and-psychopathology/article/ div-classtitlethe-snowball-effect-friendship-moder ates-escalations-in-depressed-affect-among-avoid ant-and-excluded-childrendiv/BDE31B7457DFA-120C34245A6B5296727.

Tip #17: Recognize the distraction.

1. Chance Miller, "Suspect Lawsuit Aims to Force Apple to Block Texting While Driving...Should It?" 9to5Mac, January 18, 2017, https://9to5mac .com/2017/01/18/apple-texting-and-driving-lawsuit/.

2. "Teen Driving Study Reveals 'App and Drive' Is New Danger among Teens, New Worry for Parents," Liberty Mutual Insurance, https://libertymutualgroup

.com/about-lm/news/news-release-archive/articles/
app-and-drive.

3. "Distracted Driving Public Opinion Poll," National
Safety Council, March 2016, http://www.nsc.org/
NewsDocuments/2016/DD-Methodology-Summary-
033116.pdf.

4. Sam Fox, "Teen Kills 10-Year-Old Girl and Father
of 3 While Texting and Driving," *AOL*, October 20,
2015, https://www.aol.com/article/2015/10/20/teen-
kills-10-year-old-girl-and-father-of-3-while-texting-
and-d/21251526/.

5. "Teen Charged with Manslaughter in Texting While
Driving Case," KCTV (Kansas City, MO), April 19,
2012, http://www.kctv5.com/story/17587020/teen-
charged-with-manslaughter-in-texting-while-driv
ing-case.

6. Emilie Eaton, "Lawsuit: San Antonio Teen Was
Texting While Driving, Causing Man's Death," mySA
(San Antonio), November 14, 2016, http://www
.mysanantonio.com/news/local/article/Lawsuit-San-
Antonio-teen-was-texting-while-10613468.php.

7. "Iowa Considering Stricter Offense for Texting and
Driving," *Coralville Courier*, January 20, 2017, http://
www.coralvillecourier.com/2017/01/iowa-consider
ing-stricter-offense-for-texting-and-driving.html.

8. Michael Austin, "Texting and Driving: How Dangerous Is It?" *Car and Driver*, June 2009, http://www
.caranddriver.com/features/texting-while-driving-
how-dangerous-is-it-the-results-page-2.

Tip #18: I see London, I see France.

1. Carter Coyle, "Piedmont Teen Regrets Topless Picture after It Appears on Instagram," Fox8 (High Point, NC), February 21, 2014, http://myfox8 .com/2014/02/21/piedmont-teen-regrets-topless-pic ture-after-it-appears-on-instagram/.

2. Gabrielle Chung, "Kylie Jenner: 'I Always Regret' Posting Sexy Photos," *Celebuzz,* April 11, 2016, http://www.celebuzz.com/2016-04-11/kylie-jenner-sexy-photos-marie-claire-adweek-social-media/.

3. "She's Getting Naughtier! Kim Kardashian Launches Line of. . .Phone Cases with Send Nudes Hearts on Them," *Daily Mail.com*, June 16, 2016, http://www .dailymail.co.uk/tvshowbiz/article-3645448/Kim-Kardashian-launches-line-wrapping-paper-butt-emojis-phone-cases-Send-Nudes-hearts-them.html.

4. Alex McKechnie, "Majority of Minors Engage in Sexting, Unaware of Harsh Legal Consequences," *Drexel Now*, June 18, 2014, http://drexel.edu/now/ archive/2014/June/Sexting-Study/#sthash.sT8Soj9J .dpuf.

5. Ibid.

6. Heide Splete, "Teens Who Sext Have More Sex," *Pediatric News*, July 3, 2012, http://www.mdedge.com/ pediatricnews/article/55147/pediatrics/teens-who-sext-have-more-sex.

Tip #19: No secrets.

1. George Gao, "On Social Media, Mom and Dad Are Watching," Pew Research Center, April 10, 2015, http://www.pewresearch.org/fact-tank/2015/04/10/ on-social-media-mom-and-dad-are-watching/.

Tip #20: Sleep matters.

1. "Sleepy Connected Americans," National Sleep Foundation, March 7, 2011, https://sleepfoundation.org/media-center/press-release/annual-sleep-america-poll-exploring-connections-communications-technology-use-.

2. Ruthann Richter, "Among Teens, Sleep Deprivation an Epidemic," Stanford Medicine News Center, October 8, 2015, https://med.stanford.edu/news/all-news/2015/10/among-teens-sleep-deprivation-an-epidemic.html.

3. "Study: Children Sleep Better When Parents Establish Rules, Limit Technology and Set a Good Example," National Sleep Foundation, March 3, 2014, https://sleepfoundation.org/media-center/press-release/national-sleep-foundation-2014-sleep-america-poll-finds-children-sleep.

4. Yolanda Reid Chassiakos, Jenny Radesky, Dimitri Christakis, Megan A. Moreno, and Corinn Cross, "Children and Adolescents and Digital Media," *Pediatrics* 138, no. 5 (November 2016), http://pediatrics.aappublications.org/content/138/5/e20162593.

5. Rebecca Jacobson, "Sleep Problems Have the Same Effects on Students' Grades as Drug Abuse, New Study Finds," *PBS NewsHour*, June 2, 2014, http://www.pbs.org/newshour/rundown/sleep-problems-effects-students-grades-drug-abuse-new-study-finds/.

6. Drake Baer, "An Insane Number of Teens Are Literally Losing Sleep over Social Media," Science of Us, January 17, 2017, http://nymag.com/scienceofus/

2017/01/tons-of-teens-are-literally-losing-sleep-over-social-media.html.

7. "Smartphones and Tablets in Bedrooms Disrupt Sleep Even When Switched Off," *The Telegraph*, October 31, 2016, http://www.telegraph.co.uk/sci ence/2016/10/31/smartphones-and-tablets-in-bed rooms-disrupt-sleep-even-when-swit/.

8. Victor C. Strasburger and Marjorie J. Hogan, "Children, Adolescents, and the Media," *Pediatrics* 132, no. 5 (November 2013), http://pediatrics.aappublications .org/content/132/5/958.

9. Patti Verbanas, "Texting at Night Affects Teens' Sleep, Academic Performance," *Rutgers Today*, January 22, 2016, http://news.rutgers.edu/research-news/tex ting-night-affects-teens%E2%80%99-sleep-academ ic-performance/20160121#.WIek4ZInY7U.

Tip #21: Look up.

1. "Their Last Selfie Caught the Killer That They Didn't See," *GodVine*, http://www.godvine.com/read/ their-last-selfie-caught-the-killer-that-they-didn-t- see-1516.html.

2. Elliot Rosenhaus, "10 Horrific Deaths Caused by Cell Phones," Listverse, http://listverse .com/2016/03/25/10-horrific-deaths-caused-by- smartphones/.

3. Ibid.

4. Ibid.